Whykickamoocow

Whykickamoocow

curious new zealand place names

Nicola McCloy

RANDOM HOUSE
NEW ZEALAND

For Uncle Des

A catalogue record for this book is available from the National Library of New Zealand

A RANDOM HOUSE BOOK
published by
Random House New Zealand
18 Poland Road, Glenfield, Auckland, New Zealand
www.randomhouse.co.nz

First published 2006

© 2006 Nicola McCloy

The moral rights of the author have been asserted

ISBN-13: 978 1 86941 807 6
ISBN-10: 1 86941 807 7

Design: Nick Turzynski
Cover design: Katy Yiakmis
Cover photos: sign by Chris Coad; pastoral scene Focus New Zealand Photo Library; author photo by Brian McCloy
Other photographs as credited on page 111
Printed in China

Contents

Introduction 9

First Names 10

Russell 12

Miranda 13

Gabriel's Gully 14

Helensville 15

Young Nicks Head 16

Arthur's Pass 17

Shannon 18

Ngatimoti 20

Alexandra 21

Clarence 22

Geraldine 23

Clive 25

Ross 26

Clyde 27

Global Villages 30

Milford 32

Brighton 34

Oxford 35

Cambridge 36

Coromandel 37

Fairlie 38

Jerusalem 40

Bethlehem 41

Wimbledon 42

Bombay 44

Omaha 45

Oddities 46
Utiku 48
Cape Soucis 49
Parakai 50
Neudorf 51
Taumata 52
Ophir 54
Paihia 55
Dannevirke 56
Feilding 58
Franz Josef 59
Erewhon 60

Double Meanings 62
Ward 64
Hinds 65
Bulls 66
Kumara 68
Punakaiki 69
Nightcaps 70
Raglan 72
Gore 73
Huia 75

Cityscape 76
Auckland 78
Hamilton 80
Wellington 80
Christchurch 82
Dunedin 83
Invercargill 84

Double the fun 86

Havelock/
Havelock North 88

Waimate/
Waimate North 89

Kinloch 90

Lake Rotoiti 93

Palmerston/
Palmerston North 94

The Shag Factor 96

Waipu 98

Mount Tarawera 100

Urewera 101

Tutaekuri River 102

Blackball 103

Pigroot 104

Dagg Sound 105

Cape Foulwind 106

Shag River 107

Bibliography 109

Acknowledgements
and image credits 111

Introduction

Waikikamukau . . . that's where my grandfather used to tell people he had been when he came to New Zealand on holiday. I've also been guilty of recounting an elaborate tale involving a kitten and a bulldozer when the name Kilmog has come under discussion.

While there's not really a town dedicated to booting bovines, or a hill that celebrates cat flattening, there are plenty of New Zealand places that have fascinating stories behind their names. This collection reveals the tales behind 70 of these placenames, from Waimate North to Invercargill. They tell of the lives of pre-European Maori, the arrival of European explorers, the establishment of mission stations, the first British, French and German settlers, the New Zealand Wars and the gold rushes.

The earliest of the names was given just after the arrival of the great migration from Hawaiki. The most recent was in the 1950s, when a politician and his business partner established a brand new town. The stories vary from the obvious to the obscure, but together they provide a snapshot of the history of this country.

You're invited to a dinner party and here's the rest of the invite list: Russell and Miranda, Gabriel and Helen, Nick and Arthur, Shannon and Timoti, Alexandra and Clarence, Geraldine and Clive, Ross and Clyde. What do they all have in common? They're all the names of New Zealand places, and here's how they came about . . .

Russell

It's hard to believe that the idyllic Bay of Islands town of Russell was once known as 'the hell-hole of the Pacific'. The town was originally known as Kororareka (which translates as 'how sweet is the penguin') and it provided a safe anchorage for sailors, whalers and sealers in the Far North. The laws of supply and demand meant that it soon became renowned as a den of booze and loose women.

After the signing of the Treaty of Waitangi in 1840 the leaders of the colony looked to establish a new capital for New Zealand. While Kororareka was the obvious choice, the Governor, Lieutenant William Hobson, baulked at the idea of establishing the capital in such a lawless place. He decided to build a new capital just seven kilometres to the south, at Okiato. The name of the town would be Russell.

Hobson named the town after Lord John Russell, a British politician renowned for his liberal views. Russell was to serve twice as the British prime minister, and he was noted for his support of parliamentary reform and religious freedom, and his attempts to mediate with the United States during their war for independence. On the downside, Russell was also prime minister when Britain entered the Crimean War, and during the Irish potato famine. He was also the grandfather of the British philosopher Bertrand Russell.

Meanwhile, back in New Zealand, despite Hobson's efforts to build a new capital, the colonial powers in Australia decided it should be established at Auckland. This was the death knell for Hobson's new settlement of Russell. However, Kororareka continued to thrive, and it gradually assumed the name Russell.

Miranda

The Firth of Thames hosts thousands of international visitors every year. Some of these visitors come from as far as 10,000 kilometres away, and none of them pass through Customs. With nearly 9000 hectares of tidal flats and vast tracts of mangroves, the Firth of Thames provides an ideal resting place for migratory wading birds.

With sixty different bird species in the area, the Miranda Shore Bird Centre has been set up to study the region's bird population — which includes godwits, turnstones, wrybills and red-necked stints. While the birds may have strange names, just who was Miranda and how did her name end up immortalised in a seaside town on the Firth of Thames?

In fact it wasn't a woman who gave her name to the town of Miranda but a ship. On 16 November 1863, 900 men left Auckland for the Firth of Thames. Their task was to develop forts that would provide supplies for British soldiers fighting in the Waikato in what would become known as the New Zealand Wars. Heading the fleet carrying these forces were two naval corvettes, HMS *Esk* and HMS *Miranda*. The latter carried 300 men from the 70th (Surrey) Regiment, led by Lieutenant Colonel Mulock. After spending eight days weather-bound in the Waiheke Passage, the ships finally managed to anchor just off a headland they named after HMS *Miranda*.

Several redoubts, or forts, were built in the area. One was named after the *Esk*, one after Surrey — the regiment's home base — and one after the *Miranda*. With both a headland and a redoubt named after the *Miranda*, the ship's name has remained in use, and a town has developed in the area where the redoubt was built. While Miranda's origins were militaristic and based on the colonists' desire for land, it has since made its name as a centre of excellence in conservation and caring for the environment.

Gabriel's Gully

The name Gabriel's Gully probably doesn't mean a lot to most New Zealanders nowadays, but in 1861 it was the most famous place in the country. People from all over the world arrived in New Zealand to visit the gully, and the events that took place there irrevocably changed the future of this young country.

No one is quite sure where or when Gabriel Read was born — probably Tasmania, maybe 1825. What we do know is that he loved adventure, and spent time trading in the Pacific and goldmining in Australia and California before he arrived at Port Chalmers in 1861 in search of his fortune. Gold had been discovered in a couple of places in Otago, and Read headed inland to the Tuapeka district. It wasn't long before he made a huge discovery — gold 'shining like the stars in Orion on a dark frosty night'. He made his find on 23 May 1861, informed the superintendent of the province on 28 June, and by August the entire area had been designated an official goldfield.

Just a year after Read had discovered gold the population of the Tuapeka goldfield was 11,500 — twice that of Dunedin. Otago was in the throes of massive gold rushes, which saw the country's economy boom, immigrant numbers skyrocket and the infrastructure of the South Island develop rapidly.

Gabriel Read left the Tuapeka field before the main rushes hit, in search of gold in other parts of Otago. Behind him he left a lasting legacy — the gully where he found gold carries his name to this day.

Helensville

Situated next to the Kaipara River and near the Kaipara Harbour, Helensville is a true timber town. Not just any timber either — Helensville owes its existence to the mighty kauri.

The entire area around the Kaipara Harbour was once thick with kauri forests. In the nineteenth century the tall trees were in huge demand to be hued into masts for the sailing ships plying the waters around New Zealand and further afield. The beautiful and hardy wood was also much sought after by settlers, who were beginning to replace the tents and huts they had been living in with permanent dwellings.

Over on the east coast at Waipu, a group of Scottish settlers led by Norman McLeod had arrived via Nova Scotia and Australia and were looking to establish a church-based community in New Zealand. While the name McLeod is synonymous with Waipu, it was another family of McLeods who were responsible for the establishment of a settlement on the west coast.

In 1862, John McLeod, his wife Helen and his brother Isaac arrived in the Kaipara. They had come from Nova Scotia via the Californian goldfields. Instead of making their fortune through gold, they did it through golden timber. Soon after their arrival the McLeod brothers established a sawmill to process kauri trees, shipping them out to their markets from wharves on the harbour.

Once the mill was up and running, the McLeods decided to build a home next to it, using, of course, the local kauri. The single-storey home was, by the standards of the 1860s, impressive. It soon became known as Helen's Villa as a tribute to John McLeod's wife. Helen's Villa soon evolved into Helensville, and was adopted by the local people as the name for the whole town.

John McLeod and his wife eventually returned to Nova Scotia but their legacy remained in the town of Helensville. Isaac McLeod remained in Helensville, and his descendants live there to this day.

Young Nicks Head

A 26-hour flight from Great Britain to New Zealand seems to take forever, and that first sight of land as you fly in over Northland is exciting for any Kiwi coming home. It's hard now to imagine the excitement the early explorers, both Maori and European, must have felt on first sighting land here after months at sea.

One landmark is recorded as the first sighted by two of these early explorers. Paoa, who was captain of the *Horouta* waka, sighted the headland and named it Te Kuri a Paoa — the dog of Paoa — as a tribute to his favourite dog. However, it was the second explorer who gave it the name by which it is best known today. That explorer was Captain James Cook.

On 24 September 1769 a crewmember on board the *Endeavour* noticed some seaweed drifting past the ship. To a seasoned sailor this could only mean one thing — land was near. When the sighting was reported to the captain, Cook promised that the first person to sight land would be given a gallon of rum and the privilege of having a feature of the land named after him.

The ship was still far to the east of land but the crew, responding more to the allure of extra rum than the prospect of being geographically immortalised, kept a keen eye out for distant terra firma. It was another twelve days before Cook had to make good on his promise. At two in the afternoon on 6 October, Nicholas Young, who was the personal servant of the ship's surgeon, Joseph Banks, called 'Land!'

No one knows much about Nicholas Young apart from the fact that he was born in Fife and was around twelve years of age when he spotted the far-off New Zealand coastline from the *Endeavour*. The land he sighted was soon to become known as Poverty Bay. In bestowing the promised reward, Cook named a prominent headland on the southern end of the bay after the boy. In what was perhaps an example of seafarers' wit he named it not Nicholas Young, but instead Young Nicks Head.

Arthur's Pass

South Island Maori had several established routes between the east and west coasts of the island. These routes were crucial in enabling east coast Maori to access the bountiful pounamu of the west coast. However, when Europeans arrived they were vexed as to how to cross the Southern Alps.

When gold was discovered on the west coast the need for a permanent road between the Canterbury Plains and the goldfields became more urgent. Cantabrians wanted to share in the financial rewards the gold was providing, and they didn't enjoy watching the gold leaving the west coast by ship.

Edward Dobson, Canterbury's Provincial Engineer, employed his two sons to assist him in surveying the province. As part of their job Arthur and George Dobson prospected for coal, designed drainage systems and laid out roads. In February 1864 Tarapuhi, one of the most important Maori chiefs on the east coast, told Arthur of a pass the local Maori used to travel across the alps from east to west. Realising the possible value of the pass, the Dobson brothers headed for the alps, following Tarapuhi's instructions. The terrain was difficult and the route hard, but the brothers realised that the pass could indeed potentially provide access to the west coast.

On returning to Christchurch, George Dobson reported to his father that they were unable to find a more suitable pass than Arthur's one — and Arthur's Pass it became, with work beginning on the road from west to east in April 1855. When the road was completed many people were critical of the treacherous terrain it covered, with one critic noting that 'not even the combined talents of the whole Dobson family could reduce the height of the mountains'.

Shannon

The building of railways in the North Island was critical to the survival of farmers, sawmillers, flax-millers and traders. Railways were the economic lifeline of New Zealand in the nineteenth century. The importance of the railways can be seen in the names of a number of towns, whose development was inextricably linked with the arrival of rolling stock. One of those towns is Shannon.

Lying just south of Palmerston North, Shannon was built on land that was acquired by the Wellington and Manawatu Railway Company in 1881. The company was in the process of linking Wellington and Palmerston North with a private railway. Line planning initially missed Shannon, but once the company acquired land in the area

the engineers revisited their plans and the line's present route was decided upon. On 8 March 1887 an auction of sections in the new town was held. In keeping with the railway theme, the town was named after a Wellington businessman, G.V. Shannon, who was one of the founders of the Wellington and Manawatu Railway Company.

While the railway company no longer exists and the lines it used to run have now been integrated into the Wellington commuter system and the main trunk line, the Wellington and Manawatu Railway Company left a significant legacy. They introduced the concept of on-train dining cars to New Zealand travellers, they were the first railway in the country to introduce electric lighting on passenger trains, and they gave us the town of Shannon.

Ngatimoti

A small town in the Motueka district goes by the name of Ngatimoti. Never met a person whose first name is Ngatimoti? Reckon Ngatimoti sounds like the name of a Maori tribe? Some people might look at the name Ngatimoti and see it as a tribal name — like Ngatiporou — but there is no known tribe called Moti in the Motueka region or anywhere else in New Zealand.

In the mid-1800s European missionaries came to the region and set about converting local Maori to Christianity. Once the people converted they often took, or were given, names from the Bible. One such convert took the name Timothy or, in Maori, Timoti.

In order to indicate his possession of a tree in the area, Timoti carved his name onto it. The words he carved were 'Na Timoti' — 'belonging to Timoti'. As he had staked his claim on the area, other

Maori used the name to indicate Timoti's tree. When Europeans began to settle on the land around the tree, they mistook Na Timoti for the Maori name of the district. They wrongly decided that 'na' should in fact be 'nga', and the name Ngatimoti remains in use to this day.

Alexandra

Most New Zealanders know Alexandra for its regular appearance on television weather reports as the warmest place in the country. But those who know the town well, know it simply as Alex — home of the blossom festival, the clock on the hill and possibly the best little cricket ground in the country, in Molyneux Park. This casual use of a shortened nickname simply wouldn't have done when addressing the Alexandra in honour of whom the central Otago town was named.

Alexandra owes its existence to the discovery of gold in the surrounding area in 1862. Thousands of prospectors swarmed to work the Manuherikia and Molyneux (now Clutha) rivers, and the township was born. What to call the burgeoning town was a topic of much discussion, and it was variously known as Lower Township, Junction and Manuherikia. Then, in 1863, there was a wedding.

On 10 March 1863, Albert Edward, Prince of Wales, married a Danish princess, Alexandra Carolina Marie Charlotte Louise Julia. Although she was known to her family as Alix, everyone else knew her as 'Your Highness' and later in life, when her husband became king, 'Your Majesty'. The marriage saw the young Danish beauty become the Princess of Wales. (In an interesting coincidence, the princess's husband later had an affair with Alice Keppel, who was an ancestor of the current Prince of Wales' wife, the former Camilla Parker-Bowles.)

In 1863, news of a glamorous royal wedding was a welcome distraction from the grind of life on the goldfields. The people of Manuherikia decided their town's name had changed often enough, and as a mark of respect to their new princess they would name the town after her — Alexandra.

Clarence

The Clarence River in Marlborough is named after a member of the British royal family whose love life would have sent today's tabloid newspapers into a spin.

The river rises in the Spenser Mountains, flows between the inland and seaward Kaikoura Ranges, and reaches the sea about 50 kilometres north of Kaikoura. Local Maori called it Waiautoa, which means male river. The Dillon River, which also rises in the Spenser Mountains, was known as the Waiauuha, which means female river. The two rivers are believed to have been lovers who drifted apart.

The European name Clarence came into regular use in the 1850s, with a local runholder, Francis Weld, naming the Waiautoa River after the Duke of Clarence, who became Britain's King William IV in 1830. Although the king died in 1837, Weld saw fit to commemorate him when naming the Marlborough river.

William IV is usually remembered for the reforms that took place during his reign — among them the abolition of slavery, the restriction of child labour and the restructuring of the electoral system. However, it was as Duke of Clarence that he would have challenged the current British royal family in the tabloid stakes.

In 1791, at the age of 26, the Duke met an Irish actress who went by the stage name Mrs Jordan. Her real name was Dorothea Bland. The pair embarked on an affair that was to last twenty years and result in the birth of at least ten children. The children, who went by the name FitzClarence, were not acknowledged by the Crown and did not have a place in the royal family. The affair ended in 1811, and the Duke married a German princess seven years later.

The Duke had no expectations of ascending the throne, but in 1830, after both his older brothers had died leaving no children, he became king. His two legitimate children both died before they were one year old, and when William died his niece, Victoria, became queen.

Geraldine

As a young man, James Edward Fitzgerald was acutely aware of the poverty experienced by his compatriots during the great famine in Ireland. He believed that one way to try and alleviate some of their suffering was for the Irish to emigrate in numbers to the new colonies.

Fitzgerald would have been proud of the riches that the Canterbury town named in his honour now provides. Geraldine is the home of top-notch cheesemakers at Mount Talbot, the fruit products of Barkers, and the area is renowned for its lush farmland and well-stocked salmon fisheries.

In 1854 the town's first resident, Samuel Hewlings, built a bark hut on what is now known as Talbot St. When their first child was born Hewlings and his wife Nga Hei marked the occasion by planting a totara tree, and that tree now towers above Geraldine's main street. By the time Hewlings built his hut, James Fitzgerald had been living

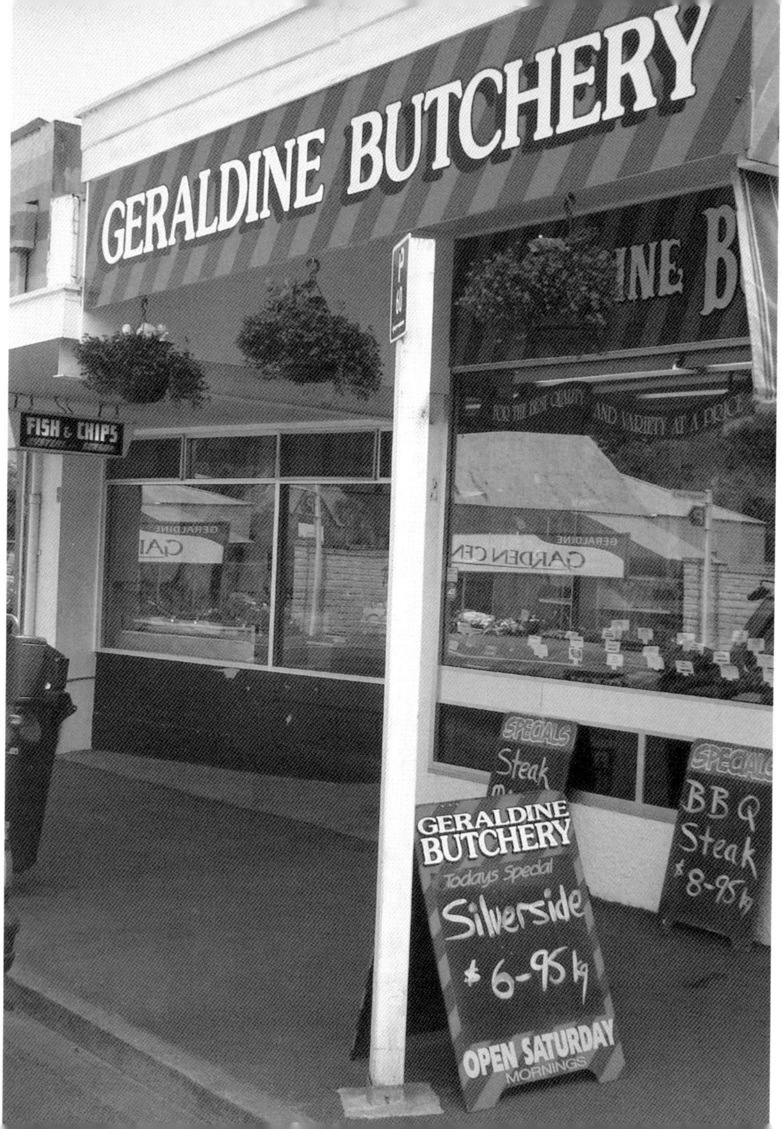
GERALDINE BUTCHERY
FISH & CHIPS
SPECIALS
Steak
GERALDINE BUTCHERY
Todays Special
Silverside
$6-95 kg
OPEN SATURDAY
MORNINGS
SPECIALS
BBQ
Steak
$8-95 kg

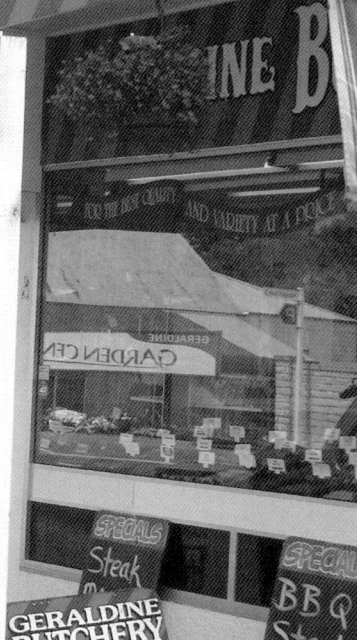

in Christchurch for almost four years and had been Superintendent of Canterbury for a year. During his time as head of the province Canterbury's population doubled, roads were built and Christ's College was opened. In 1857, suffering from ill-health, Fitzgerald resigned from public office.

In order to mark Fitzgerald's contribution to the Canterbury region, the provincial council decided to rename the town of Talbot Forest, changing the name to Fitzgerald. Two days after they made this decision, the man himself persuaded them that the town should be called Geraldine, an Irish variation of the Superintendent's family name. The chained monkey on the town's coat of arms is also a nod to Fitzgerald as it features on the family's coat of arms.

While James Fitzgerald died in Wellington in 1896, the town that became his namesake continues to go from strength to strength. It now has some 2500 residents, and immortalisation in an Exponents song.

Clive

Clive is part of Hastings district, but it lies at the point where Hastings and Napier meet. Like many towns in the Hawke's Bay area, it was named after a figure who was significant in the establishment of the British government in India.

The Indian links originated with a man called John Curling, who was Member of Parliament for Napier in 1860 and later served as a magistrate in Hastings. Curling had known Sir Charles Napier, after whom the city of Napier is named, in India. Having spent time in the subcontinent, John Curling set about ensuring that the men who were fighting to establish British ascendancy in India were commemorated here in New Zealand.

Clive of New Zealand was given its name in homage to the man known as Clive of India. Robert Clive first went to India at the age of eighteen, at a time when India was being fought over by England and France. He began work as a civil servant, but soon joined the armed forces. Clive helped to establish British influence throughout much of India during the mid-eighteenth century. He was most famous for his defence of Arcot when, leading a force of just 500, he managed to hold off some 10,000 men. This is seen by many as one of the key moments in the establishment of British control in India.

Robert Clive left India in 1767 and moved to London, but he struggled with life there, and in 1774 he committed suicide. Less than a century later, on the other side of the world, he was paid one of the ultimate compliments by John Curling and the township of Clive was born.

Ross

The name Ross is synonymous with 'the Honourable Roddy'. But who were Roddy and Ross, and why do they play an important part in South Island history?

The name Honourable Roddy was given to the biggest nugget of gold yet to be found in New Zealand. The massive nugget weighed in at around 2800 grams — worth nearly $85,000 at today's prices. It was found in 1909 in Jones Creek, a waterway that runs through a town called Ross, which is just south of Hokitika on the west coast of the South Island.

Ross is very much a gold town. After the discovery of the elusive element in 1865, a 'canvas town' sprang up on a terrace next to Jones

Creek. The nascent town was originally named Georgetown, but the name was changed to Rosstown, and then just Ross. While many towns go through several name changes before the final one is settled on, in this case all three names originated with the same man.

George Ross was an immigrant from Scotland who arrived in Lyttelton in 1851. It wasn't long before he became deeply involved in local politics and was appointed Clerk of the Provincial Council. Despite persistent ill-health Ross bought and ran several sheep stations in Canterbury, represented Rakaia as an MP, and fathered eight children. In 1865 he became Provincial Treasurer of Canterbury, and it was in honour of this office that his name, in its various forms, was bestowed on Ross. Just two years later he suffered a breakdown and bankruptcy and was forced to give up public office.

This change in fortunes was to be mirrored in the town named after George Ross. The bulk of the town's wealth was tied up in goldmining, and when large-scale mining ended in 1917 the future of the town looked a little bleak. However, Ross has survived, and today the town's industry revolves around sawmilling, farming and tourism, as people come to see the place where the Honourable Roddy was pulled from the earth.

Clyde

Throughout the 1980s it seemed scarcely a news broadcast went by without some mention of the Clyde dam project. The concrete behemoth dominates the landscape in much the same way as the river it spans dominated the landscape of the 1800s.

In 1862 Horatio Hartley and Christopher Riley discovered gold in

Whykickamoocow

the Clutha River and several settlements soon sprang up on its banks. The main administrative town for the Dunstan goldfields was initially known as Upper Dunstan, while Alexandra was called Lower Junction. The town was also called Hartley township for a time in recognition of one of the men who first found gold. Eventually, though, Upper Dunstan became known as Clyde. The thinking behind this change is unclear, but there are two possible reasons behind the name.

The first is that it was named after the River Clyde that runs through Glasgow. Giving this idea some credence is the fact that the name Clutha is a Gaelic form of the name Clyde. Clutha is thought to mean 'strength of the water current', which given the swift, swirling nature of the Clutha seems appropriate.

A second possibility is that the town was named after Field Marshal Sir Colin Campbell, who was also Lord Clyde. He was a Scottish military leader who gave distinguished service in the British army, especially in India where he was involved in the relief of the city of Lucknow during the Indian rebellion in 1857.

Whatever the origin of its name, Clyde has survived the boom and bust of the gold-rush years, the move of the administrative centre of the region to Alexandra, and the building of the giant dam right on its doorstep. Despite all the hardship the town has been through it remains one of the most attractive towns in Central Otago.

A trip to Bombay or Bethlehem would involve a long-haul flight, a passport and multiple time zones, right? Wrong. You can visit a whole pile of international towns without even leaving the country. England, Scotland, Wales, India, Israel and the United States — while this list looks like it could be a holiday itinerary or a military alliance, it is in fact a list of nations whose towns share names with places in New Zealand.

Global Villages

Milford

When the name Milford was attached to a fiord on the South Island's west coast, it probably had a bit in common with its Welsh namesake. Both have deep-water harbours, and both hosted early whaling stations. As the years have passed, however, the two places could not have become more different.

Milford Sound was originally called Milford Haven after the port town in Pembrokeshire. It didn't take long before the Haven was dropped and it became known as Milford Sound.

Just who named the Sound is unclear. One theory says it was Captain Stokes, who owned land on the banks of Milford Haven. He is known to have left a number of Welsh names in his wake, including the Cleddau River and Pembroke Peak. Another possibility is that Captain Peter Williams decided to honour his home town of Milford Haven. A third Welshman, Captain John Grono, is also a contender.

Whoever it was that named the Sound, they couldn't have imagined how different these two Welsh and New Zealand places would become. Milford Haven's status as a whaling town saw it develop into an important port for Wales. Oil has also become vital to the town, and its primary industry is now oil refining. The deep-water harbour has become a well-used shipping channel, playing host to a continual stream of oil tankers, ferries and container ships.

Meanwhile Milford Sound has taken the opposite tack. With its whaling stations gone, it is now part of one of the last great wilderness areas in the world. Its main industry is tourism, and its lush rainforest, bountiful wildlife and thundering waterfalls are protected as part of Fiordland National Park.

Brighton

English seaside resorts — while to some people this phrase seems an oxymoron, the English love their seaside towns. And while we haven't adopted their rented deckchairs, tooth-breaking rock and knotted handkerchiefs in New Zealand, we have adopted some of their resort names.

Just south of Dunedin is a town that once boasted a rather plain name — Boat Harbour. An early resident of Boat Harbour, Hugh Williams, decided the town needed a name that better reflected the nature of the beach village. The name he chose was Brighton, in homage to one of the best known British seaside resorts.

The original Brighton lies on the south coast of Sussex about two hours from London. It has been inhabited since 3500BC, and in Anglo-Saxon times it was called Beorthelm's-tun, meaning Beorthelm's town. Brighton also features in the Domesday book under the name Bristemestune. By 1514 it was called Brighthelmstone, a name that persisted until the mid-eighteenth century. It was then that sea bathing became fashionable and Brighthelmstone reinvented itself as Brighton, seaside resort.

Back on this side of the world, Brighton near Dunedin (like New Brighton in Christchurch) became an established seaside town. When cars began to become part of the early twentieth century landscape, well-off Dunedinites would motor out to Brighton to enjoy a day by the sea. While today it is a short drive to Brighton, at that time it was about as far as you could comfortably drive for a day trip. But one thing hasn't changed — on a hot summer day Brighton beach is a beautiful place to be.

Oxford

The bush camp turned town has a very short history compared to the city of dreaming spires from which it takes its name. While the British Oxford was built on the world of academia and boasts the oldest university in the English-speaking world, the New Zealand version has its roots firmly in the soil — first as a sawmilling town and later as a farming centre.

Milling began in Harewood Forest in North Canterbury in 1852. The men who felled the timber and worked the mill established a bush camp on the edge of the forest. By 1859 surveyor Thomas Cass was reporting that a village had formed out of the original camp, and by 1861 the new town was named Oxford. It is unclear whether the early Cantabrians bestowed the name as an acknowledgement of the support Samuel Wilberforce, the Bishop of Oxford, gave to the Canterbury Association or if it was a nod to the fact that many members of the association were educated at the colleges of Oxford.

The English city of Oxford first appears in written records nearly 950 years before its New Zealand counterpart, in the year 912. It was initially known as Oxenaforda and was established as a nunnery by St Frideswide some time in the eighth century. The university of Oxford dates back to the 1200s, with the establishment of University College, Balliol and Merton, all of which are still in existence to this day.

Along with the town of Oxford, Canterbury is strewn with references to the university and its students. The most notable is the city of Christchurch, named by old Oxonian John Robert Godley after his former college, while a fellow Oxford student, J.H. Cust, gave his name to the nearby town of Cust.

Cambridge

Cambridge, south of Hamilton, is one of New Zealand's most English towns. While its tree-lined streets and village square echo its English past, the peaceful nature of the town belies its birth through war.

The Waikato was the scene of some of the bloodiest fighting in the New Zealand Wars. A year after their invasion of the Waikato in 1863, the British army decided to build a redoubt on what had been the site of Horotiu pa. The fort, known as Ten Star Redoubt, was home to over a thousand soldiers involved in the war in the Waikato. The site was chosen since its position on the banks of the Waikato River meant gunboats could bring men and supplies up the river to the settlement.

At the end of hostilities many of the British soldiers were allotted an acre of land in town as well as some farmland. A village soon grew up around what had been a pa and then a fort. The settlement was soon given the name Cambridge.

Whether it was named directly after the town in Britain is unknown. It has been suggested that the Waikato River reminded some of the River Cam, which runs through Cambridge. It may also have been named after the Duke of Cambridge who was commander-in-chief of the British army during the New Zealand Wars.

Regardless of the reason behind its name, Cambridge is linked inextricably with the town of the same name in England. The famed university town was originally called Grantebryge, with the river that ran through it called the Granta. Over the centuries the name has morphed into Cambridge. The river is still sometimes called the Granta, but its name has also changed to the Cam, to match that of the town.

Coromandel

To most New Zealanders the name Coromandel is synonymous with summers by the beach. The town and the peninsula that bear the name are holiday havens for North Islanders, who love the relaxed lifestyle the Coromandel has to offer.

Coromandel takes its name from HMS *Coromandel*, a British Navy storeship that anchored off the peninsula in June 1820. The ship spent a year based in the Hauraki Gulf before sailing back to England loaded with kauri timber. The town that took the ship's name became the peninsula's major port, serving the area's gold and kauri timber industries. So significant was the town to the region that the entire peninsula took its name.

HMS *Coromandel* got its name from another Coromandel Coast — the southeastern coast of India. The coast is home to Chennai — or Madras, as it was known to the British — and the French enclave of Pondicherry. While the origins of the name Coromandel are unclear, it is thought to have come from the Tamil phrase 'Chola Mandal'. The Chola was a dynasty that ruled southern India, while 'mandalam' is a Tamil term meaning 'the region'. The North Island's coastal gem is therefore 'the region of the Chola dynasty of south India'.

It is hard to imagine that the two Coromandel coasts could have much in common, but in fact they do. Like its New Zealand namesake, the Indian Coromandel has lush farmland, native forest and plentiful natural resources. Both the Indian and New Zealand coasts are home to significant mangrove wetlands and, like the Firth of Thames, the Indian coastline is home to thousands of migrating birds.

Fairlie

The town of Fairlie in South Canterbury owes its name to a romantic pair of Scottish settlers who arrived in the area in 1866.

David Hamilton had been living in New York when he met his wife-to-be, Margaret. She is rumoured to have moved to New York to avoid her parents' plans to marry her off to a cousin. The pair married in the United States in 1859 but returned to their home country of Scotland for their honeymoon. They spent their first weeks as newlyweds in the charming village of Fairlie, on the North Ayrshire coast. Although they emigrated to New Zealand the following year, the pair never forgot the time they had spent looking out across the sea to Cumbraes and the Isle of Arran.

In 1866 they settled in South Canterbury with Margaret's brother and his wife. Soon after moving to the area they established a boarding house and a post office. Along with the post office came the inevitable quandary of what to call the new settlement. Their first choice was Hamilton but this, they decided, would get confused with the town of the same name in the Waikato.

After some thought, David and Margaret chose the name Fairlie Creek, in memory of the town where they had spent their honeymoon. The post office, and thus the settlement, took the name Fairlie Creek, but in 1892 this was shortened to Fairlie.

Global Villages

Jerusalem

The histories of both the New Zealand and the Middle Eastern towns of Jerusalem have been almost entirely dominated by one thing — religion. Jerusalem, or Hiruharama, on the banks of the Whanganui River, shares its name with the biblical city. The New Zealand version was blessed with its name by an early English missionary, Richard Taylor, who arrived in the region in 1843. He quickly became established as a peacekeeper and converted some two-thirds of the area's Maori to Christianity.

The Middle Eastern town of Jerusalem, after which Taylor named the river town, has been in existence since at least 3000BC. It is an important religious site for Christians, Jews and Muslims alike. The town's name is thought to be derived from the Hebrew Yerushalayim. 'Yerusha' translates as heritage, while the second half of the name could derive from 'shalem' which means harmony, or 'shalom' which means peace. Therefore Jerusalem can be translated as Heritage of Peace.

The name is appropriate for the town on the Whanganui River, where Richard Taylor played a key part in maintaining peace among local Maori. Forty years after Taylor arrived on the river, the Catholic mission there became home to Mother Mary Aubert. She established a religious community in Jerusalem to provide health care and education. The community remains there to this day.

The poet James K. Baxter moved there in 1969. He established a community that he hoped would live without money or books, existing to worship God and work the land. The community was racked with problems, however, and Baxter's health suffered. But after his death in August 1972 his body was returned to the place where he had found peace — Jerusalem.

Bethlehem

Every year at Christmas one small New Zealand post office is deluged with mail because people want its special postmark on their Christmas cards. That post office is in Bethlehem, once a town in its own right, now a suburb of Tauranga.

Like its namesake in the Middle East, Bethlehem in the Bay of Plenty has a history that includes war and dispossession. The town got its name from Christian missionaries who were working in the region to try and help resettle the many Maori whose land had been confiscated during the New Zealand Wars. It is known to local Ngati Ranginui Maori as Peterehema, the Maori form of Bethlehem.

The missionaries named the town Bethlehem after the city that, according to the gospels, was the birthplace of Jesus. Since the birth of the Messiah, the city has been under the rule of followers of Islam, Christianity and Judaism, and it remains home to significant populations from each of these religions. The name Bethlehem is derived from the Hebrew term 'Beth-lehem', meaning house of bread, although the town has experienced more than its share of hunger and strife. The name is perhaps more suited to the New Zealand town, situated as it is in the Bay of Plenty.

While New Zealand's Bethlehem has faced losing its identity by being swallowed up by the city of Tauranga, the original Bethlehem has faced being lost through some of the most violent fighting seen in the twentieth century. With the partition of Palestine in 1947 Bethlehem came under the administration of the United Nations, but this only lasted until 1948, when Jordan occupied the city. The Jordanian occupation continued until 1967, when Israel recaptured the city. In 1995 control of the city moved again, when it was ceded to the newly established Palestinian Authority. Its future, like that of much of the region, remains uncertain.

Wimbledon

Once a year, tennis fans all over the world tune in to a tournament that has links to a small town in Hawke's Bay. While Pimms and strawberries are the order of the day at Wimbledon in London, Wimbledon in Hawke's Bay is more of a pint and pie town. The two towns are, however, inextricably linked.

The story behind the name of the Hawke's Bay town is one of dubious origins. According to a Dannevirke publican, it goes something like this: some time in the 1880s one of the locals shot a cattle beast that was quite a distance away from him. A wag who saw him take the shot called out, 'That was good enough for Wimbledon!'

Confused? Not sure what getting a good shot on a bull has to do with tennis? Well, back in the nineteenth century, the British rifle-shooting championships were held at Wimbledon. It was not until the early twentieth century that Wimbledon became associated with lawn tennis.

The actual meaning of the name Wimbledon is unclear. The name has only been in constant use for two hundred years, despite there being evidence of habitation right back to the Iron Age. In 967 the town was called Wimbedounyg, which would have given rise to the curious 'Wombles of Wimbedounyg'! Over time the name gradually changed to Wimbleton, and later to its current form, Wimbledon.

Global Villages

Bombay

The Bombay Hills provide a visible and almost mythical divide between Auckland and the 'real' New Zealand, featuring in the saying that most Aucklanders have heard more than once — that there is life south of the Bombay Hills. The hills provide a physical (and some would say psychological) barrier between Auckland and the Waikato.

The hills take their name from the nearby township of Bombay, which has precious little in common with its larger Indian namesake. The town got its name from the ship *Bombay*, which brought settlers to the area between Drury and Pokeno in 1863. The ship itself was named after the huge Indian city that is capital of the state of Maharastra.

While New Zealand's Bombay was established in the 1860s, the Indian version has been inhabited since around 250BC. Our Bombay is a small village, while the Indian city is one of the five biggest metropolitan areas in the world. The original name of the city was Mumbai, a name whose origins lie in Hindu mythology. 'Mumba' is derived from the name of the Hindu goddess Mumbadevi, the patron of salt collectors and fishermen, and 'Aai' is the Marathi word for mother. However, when the Portuguese arrived in the sixteenth century they named the area Bom Bahia, meaning good bay. The name was then changed to Bombay when the English took control of the region less than a hundred years later.

Even after India became independent from Britain the name Bombay remained, until it was officially changed back to Mumbai in 1995. The Auckland town, and its well-known hills, have stuck with the Anglo-Portuguese appellation of Bombay.

Omaha

Omaha, north of Auckland, is a beachside town that is primarily populated by Aucklanders who have their holiday homes there. It shares its name with cities in the US states of Arkansas, Georgia, Illinois, Nebraska and Texas. Unlike Bombay, Jerusalem and Oxford, however, the New Zealand name comes from a very different source and means something quite different from that of its global counterparts.

The New Zealand Omaha is a Maori name that means 'place of pleasure', an extremely accurate description of a town where people go for sun, sand and relaxation. The multiple towns of Omaha in the US derive their name from a Native American tribe. The Omaha people, whose name translates as 'those going against the wind or current', originated in Iowa, but eventually settled in Nebraska.

The tribe's name came into international usage in 1944. As the Allied forces planned their assault on German-occupied mainland France, they needed to use codes when communicating possible landing sites. One of these codenames was Omaha Beach. The 5.6-kilometre-long beach was eventually chosen as one of the key landing points during the Normandy landings.

On 6 June 1944 hundreds of soldiers came ashore at Omaha Beach and secured the beach and much of the surrounding area. The Normandy landings proved to be a critical turning point in the war for the Allies. The French government later acknowledged the importance of the landings by giving official recognition to the beach's codename, and it is now called Omaha Beach.

Oddities

Placenames can have all sorts of unusual origins — there are names that are spelled backwards or jumbled, names that seem misspelled, French names, Danish names, German names, biblical names and names that tell a whole story. They're all here. The only thing the placenames in this section have in common is that they all have unusual origins.

Utiku

Just south of Taihape is the settlement of Utiku. While it might seem like just another small North Island town, Utiku owes its existence to a controversial government policy and its name to an unusual tale from the Bible.

In 1895 the Crown passed the Native Townships Act, which allowed the establishment of townships on Maori land. The land remained in Maori ownership but was leased to European settlers for periods of up to 42 years, for minimal rent. The scheme was developed to open up the North Island for settlers, and was weighted in favour of the recent arrivals rather than as a way to benefit local Maori.

Among the eighteen townships established under the Act were Tokaanu, Otorohanga, Taumarunui and Utiku. While Utiku seems at first glance to be a Maori name, it is in fact the Maori version of a name from a strange little story in the Bible.

In the book of Acts, a young man called Eutychus was sitting on the sill of a third-floor window listening to Paul speaking. Eutychus was really tired, and as he listened he nodded off, with the result that he fell out of the window to his death. He was soon brought back to life by Paul, proving that he was deserving of the name his mother had given him — Eutychus, or 'lucky'.

When the Bible was translated into Maori, the name Eutychus was turned into Utiku, the town whose name means 'lucky'.

Cape Soucis

At the entrance to Croisilles Harbour, northeast of Nelson, is Cape Soucis. The area is rife with names that hark back to France. While the influence of English and Scottish colonists can be seen throughout New Zealand, there are only a handful of places where the influence of their Gallic counterparts is in evidence. The northern coast of the South Island is one of them.

This French influence is largely down to one man — Jules Sébastien César Dumont d'Urville. In his home country d'Urville is most renowned for unearthing a statue in the Greek Islands in 1820 — that statue was the Venus de Milo, and it now stands in the Louvre in Paris.

In 1826 d'Urville set out from France on the *Astrolabe* to survey the lands of the Mare Pacificum — the South Pacific. During this expedition he and his crew encountered many of the peoples of the Great Southern Ocean. They mapped and documented the lands that came to be known as Papua New Guinea, French Polynesia and, of course, New Zealand.

While surveying the New Zealand coastline in 1827, d'Urville sailed the *Astrolabe* into an area he named Croisilles Harbour. Not long after he had crossed into the harbour the ship was becalmed, left at the mercy of turbulent currents and a threatening swell. D'Urville's description of this time was noted in the *Astrolabe*'s ship's log: 'So we passed the entire night less that three miles from the land, a prey to the most lively inquietude and dreading to be carried, in spite of ourselves, onto the coast.'

It is this experience that inspired the naming of Cape Soucis. While the word 'soucis' can mean marigolds in French, the cape of marigolds this is not. In this case the name is more aptly translated as the cape of worries or the cape of concerns, due to the inclement conditions d'Urville and his crew encountered there.

After a week on full alert, the sailors finally managed to steer their ship through the difficult and dangerous crossing that is French Pass and head toward the island that now bears their skipper's name — D'Urville Island.

Parakai

Visitors flock to the town of Parakai every year to wallow in its hot springs and relax by the Kaipara Harbour. In fact, without the hot springs there probably wouldn't be a town at Parakai.

In 1881 the Helensville Town Board took over the administration of the hot springs reserve, which was situated some three kilometres out of town. At that stage the springs were not much more than a muddy hole in the ground bubbling with hot water. It wasn't until the 1890s that a bathhouse was built and the springs were developed for public bathing.

The springs, and the settlement that grew up around them, were known as Helensville Hot Springs. Until 1908, when a boarding house was built, the many visitors to the area had to stay in nearby Helensville if they wanted to immerse themselves in the restorative waters of the springs. The year 1908 also saw the establishment of a post office in the town, and the people of Helensville Hot Springs decided that their growing settlement needed a new name.

A public meeting was called to discuss possible names, with popular opinion supporting Kaipara, after the nearby harbour and river. However, the existence of a post office at Kaipara Flats meant this suggestion had to be rejected. After giving the problem some thought, one of the women at the meeting, Mrs Robert Ferrall, came up with a possible solution to the problem: 'Why not turn the word around and make it Parakai?'

The idea appealed, and the name Parakai was adopted. While the order of the syllables in the two names — Kaipara and Parakai — has been reversed, they retain the same meaning in Maori — to eat fern roots.

Neudorf

'New town' is probably the least original of all the placenames in New Zealand. Wellington has one in the form of Newtown, while Auckland has its Newton. However, there is one new town that has infinitely more interesting origins than its big suburban counterparts.

Late in 1842, the *St Pauli* sailed out of Hamburg in Germany bringing a group of emigrants to a fresh life in New Zealand. They were headed for Nelson, where one of their number had bought six allotments from the German Colonisation Company, which was an offshoot of the New Zealand Company.

The *St Pauli* arrived in Nelson in April 1843 after a difficult journey. The new arrivals found the land allotted to them was in the Moutere Valley outside Nelson. It was covered in bush and the soil was of poor quality. They named their first settlement St Paulidorf, after the ship they had travelled on, and the valley Schachtstal, after the captain of the ship. Life in the valley was difficult, however, and after serious flooding most of the settlers abandoned the area. Eventually they resettled in new towns further up the valley. Two of these towns were Sarau (Upper Moutere) and Rosental (Rosedale). Another of the new towns was called just that — Neudorf is the German for new town.

Ironically, the poor soil that so disappointed the original immigrants is the very thing that has made Neudorf famous today. The soil is perfect for growing grapes, and wines from the region, including the Neudorf brand, are now challenging German wines on the world market.

Taumata

An otherwise unremarkable hill in southern Hawke's Bay boasts one of the most commented upon placenames in New Zealand. The hill, which is only 305 metres high, is known to locals as Taumata, but its full name is one of the longest placenames in the world.

The full name on the sign next to the hill, just out of Porangahau, is: Taumatawhakatangihangakoauauotamateaturipukakapikimaungahoronukupokaiwhenuakitanatahu

A rough translation of this is: 'The summit of the hill where Tamatea, the man with the big knees, who slid, climbed and swallowed mountains, known as Land Eater, played his nose flute to his loved one.'

There is some debate as to whether Tamatea's full name qualifies as the world's longest placename. The residents of the Welsh town of Llanfairpwllgwyngyllgogerychwyrndrobwllllantysiliogogogoch claim New Zealanders added the bit about eating mountains in order to win the title of the world's longest name. Taumatawhakatangihangakoauauotamateapokaiwhenuakitanatahu would only qualify as the second

Taumatawhakatangihangakoauauotamateaturipukakapikimaungahoronukupokaiwhenuakitanatahu

longest name. However, on this side of the world, the argument is that the longer of the names is the more formal and thus the most correct.

It seems unlikely that either town will give up its claim to having the record-holding name, but one thing is for sure — Taumata is the name with the most vowels. The Welsh name boasts a mere 13, against New Zealand's 48!

Ophir

Visit the village of Ophir in Central Otago these days and you'll find a handful of cribs, several well-restored buildings and a much-photographed post office. If you had visited Ophir in the early 1860s you would have found something completely different.

The discovery of gold in the Manuherikia River in 1862 led to the realisation that the golden hills of Central Otago were literally that — hills of gold. The Manuherikia Valley and its neighbour, the Ida Valley, were suddenly alive with prospectors, all looking for their share of the life-changing gold. By April 1863 a small town had sprung into life next to the Manuherikia River. The river's paylode had become famous, and within about three months there were several thousand people living in and near the town. Canvas tents, wooden lean-tos and mudbrick and schist huts lined the makeshift streets. Along with gold comes money, and soon the temporary settlement had become a thriving town.

The town soon had not one but two names — Blacks and Ophir. The name Blacks was from one of the original gold claims, Black's Diggings. Despite the government changing the name of the post office from Blacks to Ophir on 1 May 1875, the name Blacks lives on to this day in the form of the town's pub — the Blacks Hotel.

What of the name Ophir? Its history is an ancient one that harks right back to biblical times, as seen here in 1 Kings 22.48: 'Jehoshaphat made ships of Tharshish to go to Ophir for gold: but they went not; for the ships were broken at Ezion-geber.'

While it is highly unlikely that Jehoshaphat was headed for Central Otago, he was off in search of gold. In biblical times Ophir was a secret land where gold and precious stones were abundant. No one really knows the location of the biblical Ophir, and academics and adventurers alike try to find its whereabouts to this day. One thing we do know is that the mythical land has easily located namesakes, both of them gold towns — one in Central Otago, the other in Utah in the US.

Paihia

The great weather, good fishing, beautiful scenery and historic sites around Paihia attract thousands of visitors every year. In summer the town's population swells with campers and bach owners who head north to kick back and have a good time. After all, 'good' is what Paihia is all about.

When the first European missionaries arrived in New Zealand they struggled to communicate with Maori. One such missionary was the Reverend Henry Williams, who arrived in the Bay of Islands in 1823 to work for the Church of England's Church Mission Society. When he was training to be a missionary, Williams' superiors had criticised him for his inability to master Greek and Latin. When he arrived in New Zealand these ancient languages were about as useful to him as English, so he set about trying to learn as much of the Maori language as he could. Among the vocabulary that Williams picked up quickly was the word 'pai', meaning good.

Williams and his family were keen to set up a base in Northland, but decided against the wild and relatively lawless trading centre of Kororareka (Russell). While looking for an appropriate place to settle his family and begin his mission work, Williams came across a bay with sandy beaches and a pleasant outlook. He turned to his Maori companion and pronounced, 'It's pai here.' Williams then proceeded to build a house, store and New Zealand's first church in the spot we now know as Paihia.

Dannevirke

The recent marriage of Crown Prince Frederik of Denmark to a young Tasmanian woman brought Australia to a standstill. Here in New Zealand there was one town that took more than a passing interest in the celebrations. That town was Dannevirke.

The town owes its existence to Julius Vogel's government of the early 1870s. Under its Public Works Act, Danish settlers were recruited to help clear forest land in Hawke's Bay. They settled in an area known as Seventy Mile Bush, where they were employed clearing dense bush in order to develop farmland, and building roads and railways.

The primary settlement in Seventy Mile Bush was known as Dannevirke, a name chosen by the New Zealand government before the settlers even arrived. The term Dannevirke translates as 'Dane's work', but it also refers to a series of fortifications built in the ninth century that protected the country from invasion.

Despite the rigours of land clearing and sawmilling, the settlers

57
Oddities

soon built themselves slab huts and a town sprang up. As the land was cleared and farming and sawmilling brought money to the town the slab huts were replaced with more permanent houses. The new roads meant access to the area was much easier, and more people came to live in Dannevirke. Soon the town had established itself as a hub for the surrounding rural area.

By naming the town Dannevirke the government hoped to give the new settlers a sense of belonging in the area. It must have worked as the town still boasts a number of citizens descended from those first settlers and its people remain fiercely proud of their town's Scandinavian heritage.

Feilding

Driving through Feilding, people often wonder where the C is. No, not the sea — the town is a bit of a drive from the coast. The missing C is the one we all heard about at primary school — I before E except after C. So why is Feilding not Fielding?

Well, it all comes down to a bloke called Colonel William Henry Adelbert Feilding. The colonel was a director of a group called the Emigrants and Colonists Aid Corporation. Concerned with reducing unemployment in England, the corporation looked to the colonies to create new settlements for British emigrants. Colonel Feilding was given the task of travelling to the 'New World' and buying land for these settlements.

After rejecting possible areas of Queensland, Feilding arrived in Wellington in 1871. He then travelled to the Manawatu where he was impressed with the country, and arranged to buy 100,000 acres of land from the government for £75,000. The area became known as the 'Manchester Block'. The colonial government agreed to provide free passage for 2000 settlers over a five-year period. The first 23 of these assisted immigrants (and the founding citizens of the town named after its founder — Feilding) arrived on 22 January 1874.

Colonel Feilding was not the only member of the Emigrants and Colonists Aid Corporation to leave his stamp on the Manawatu. Look at any map of the area and you will see that Henry Ashhurst, Arthur Halcomb and the Duke of Manchester are also commemorated in the region's names.

Franz Josef

The residents of a small West Coast town should be glad they don't have to use their namesake's full title when they talk about their town and nearby glacier. If they did it would easily rival the world's longest placenames, going something like this: His Imperial and Apostolic Majesty, Franz Josef, By the Grace of God, Emperor of Austria, King of Hungary and Bohemia, King of Dalmatia, Croatia, Slavonia, Lodomeria and Illyria; King of Jerusalem, Archduke of Austria; Grand Duke of Tuscany and Kraków, Duke of Lorraine, of Salzburg, Styria, Carinthia, Carniola and of the Bukovina; Grand Prince of Transylvania . . . OK, there's more, but you get the picture.

The South Island's West Coast may seem an incongruous place to have a town and glacier named after an Austrian emperor, but that is entirely down to one man, Julius von Haast. When Haast, a German geologist, arrived in New Zealand in 1858 the country's mineral resources were just beginning to be tapped. He was soon employed in Canterbury to provide advice on the region's mineral prospects. As part of his job as provincial geologist he undertook a huge survey of the entire region, which at that time included Westland.

In 1865 Haast arrived at the impressive glacier that grinds for 13 kilometres, down from the Southern Alps out towards the coast. He named it after Franz Josef, the Emperor of Austria. While Haast was not the first European to discover the glacier, in his role of mapping the entire region he was able to give it an official name.

While the West Coast's Franz Josef is all about peace and tranquillity, the same cannot be said of its namesake. In the interests of expanding his Hapsburg empire, Franz Josef lead the nation into the Crimean War, the Austro-Sardinian war, the Austro-Prussian war and finally World War I. When it was suggested he use new technology in the form of tanks while fighting alongside Germany in the First World War, his shocked response was: 'Absolutely not. The horses will be startled.' He didn't live to see the end of the war and the break-up of his beloved empire, or indeed his tranquil and majestic namesake on the other side of the world.

Erewhon

Situated in the high country northwest of Ashburton is one of New Zealand's best-known sheep farms — Erewhon Station. The story behind the station's name begins in England in 1835 with the birth of Samuel Butler.

Despite receiving a Cambridge education and seeming to be destined to follow his father into a career in the church, Butler decided he wanted something more adventurous out of life and emigrated to New Zealand. Just ten months after his arrival Butler had traversed Canterbury in search of good sheep country. He bought several land leases near the upper reaches of the Rangitata River and established Mesopotamia Station, which in time comprised 55,000 acres. During his time at Mesopotamia, Butler established himself as a writer, with his work being published regularly by the *Press* in Christchurch. His first book was *A First Year in Canterbury Settlement*. He returned to England in 1864 — having made enough money from his four years on Mesopotamia to support him for the rest of his life — and trained as an artist while continuing to write.

In 1872, Butler's novel *Erewhon, or Over the Range* was published anonymously. It was a satirical work based in a fictional country named Erewhon, or nowhere written as an anagram. The first few chapters of the book, where the protagonist goes out in search of Erewhon, are based on Butler's own experience of exploring Canterbury. It was critically acclaimed and became a literary classic, to this day being compared to George Orwell's *1984* and Jonathan Swift's *Gulliver's Travels*.

The owners of Stonechrubie Station, one of the runs that bordered Mesopotamia, decided to commemorate Butler's novel by renaming some of the land that had inspired him to write the book, and thus today we have Erewhon Station.

Double Meanings

After the Gore she'd seen on Ward rounds, she drove home past grazing Hinds and Bulls. At home she dined on Kumara and Pancakes. After dinner she knitted a Raglan sleeve, had a couple of Nightcaps and watched a documentary about the Huia.

How many times have you seen a placename and thought, 'How on earth did it end up being called that?' Here are the answers to a handful of those questions.

Double Meanings

Ward

The word Ward can mean a number of things, none of which really make sense when it comes to naming a town — there's the hospital ward, the electoral ward, and then there's the ward of the state. All these definitions do have one thing in common, however — they are all things that rely on the government — and that's where the link with the real reason for calling a town Ward lies.

The land on which Ward is built used to be part of one of the first great sheep stations in the South Island. Called Flaxbourne, it was established in 1847 by Charles Clifford and Frederick Weld, who adds to the political nature of this tale by being one of New Zealand's early prime ministers. At its peak Flaxbourne covered over 64,000 acres (26,000 hectares) but the station was broken up into smaller runs in 1905. The land was then balloted out to settlers, which heralded the development of new towns in the area.

The people of one of these towns were keen that their settlement be called Flaxbourne but the government had other ideas. They decided to name the town after Sir Joseph Ward, the man who was minister of railways at the time. While the main trunk line runs through Ward now, at the time it hadn't quite made it to the town — that didn't happen until 1911.

After the town of Ward was named after him, Joseph Ward became prime minister, and it was under his stewardship that New Zealand made the transition from a colony to a dominion. Despite having a town in Marlborough named after him, Ward remained a Southlander to the day he died, and he is buried in the town where he grew up — Bluff.

Hinds

With the proliferation of deer farms throughout the South Island, it is perhaps not surprising that there is a town named after the female deer. Hinds, southwest of Ashburton in Canterbury, doesn't take its name from Bambi's mum though.

Like most of the early settlements in Canterbury, the town takes its name from a member of the Canterbury Association. The association was formed in London, and primarily made up of well-to-do Englishmen who wanted to develop communities in the colonies that held the Anglican faith and English civilisation at their core. Among its ranks was a Dr Samuel Hinds. A churchman all his life, Hinds strongly supported Edward Gibbon Wakefield's desire to create 'the most Church of England country in the world'.

During an address to a select committee on New Zealand settlement in the British House of Lords, Hinds expressed his support for immigration to the New World. He made it clear that he thought the British government had a right to colonise New Zealand because it had not been 'subject to civilisation'.

All the while that Samuel Hinds was involved with the Canterbury Association he was also furthering his church career. In 1844 he was appointed Dean of Carlisle, and he was promoted to the position of Bishop of Norwich in 1849. He resigned from the Norwich bishopric in 1857 and moved back to London, where he died in 1872.

Bulls

Anyone who has driven through the Manawatu town of Bulls will have noticed the signs that litter the place — outside the police station there's 'Constabull', outside the public toilets it's 'Relieveabull', and outside the church 'Forgiveabull' — but not many people know why the town has its bovine name.

James Bull was a woodworker by trade, and among other things responsible for some of the elaborate carvings in the British House of Commons before he set sail for the colonies in search of a new life. His skills were highly sought after in New Zealand, where the colonists were beginning to build houses, hotels and public buildings.

Bull first arrived in the Rangitikei region in 1858, being employed to put some finishing touches to the hotel at Scotts Ferry. The following year he leased some land off a local landowner and built a store. The store became a focal point for the community, providing the locals with a place to buy supplies, have a beer and post or pick up their mail. The business soon expanded. As well as a drink, travellers could now find a bed. On top of the postal service, Bull soon established a carrying company, and not forgetting his original trade, he set up a sawmilling company. Within five years, the people who lived near the store found they were going to Bull's for everything.

As well as building his own business, James Bull also provided the community with a courthouse and a hospital. The growing settlement had several names, including Rangitikai and Clifton, but in recognition of James Bull's contribution to the area the town was officially named Bulls.

TOWN HALL

BULLS

SOCI-A-BULL

Kumara

The origin of New Zealand's own sweet potato, the kumara, is a mystery. While it is known that the delicious tuber arrived in New Zealand along with the Maori during the great migrations, no one really knows where it originated. Some say it came from South America, some say Central America, while others reckon it's from somewhere in Asia.

Equally mysterious is how the town got the name it shares with the sweet potato. Kumara, just south of Greymouth, came into being as a result of the West Coast gold rushes in the 1870s. One of the first Europeans to settle there was a British storekeeper who went on to become one of this country's most famous leaders, Richard John Seddon.

While the town's history is well known, the origin of the name Kumara is not. A straightforward explanation would be that the local Maori gave it the name because the area provided land on which to nurture abundant kumara beds. However, this is not the case. Kumara is too far south to grow the tasty tubers. Adding to the intrigue is the fact that locals pronounce the two words quite differently — the town as Coo-*ma*-ra and the potato as *Coo*-mi-ra.

The most likely explanation is that the area was originally named Kohimara. When the surveyor Arthur Dobson arrived at the mouth of the Taramakau River he found the land covered in a blooming plant the local Maori called kohimara. Here the mystery deepens once more — kohimara has been described as a type of convolvulus, and also as a variety of bush lawyer.

The name Kohimara didn't last very long after the gold rush

brought a permanent population to the area. Whether through the difficulty of pronunciation or simple laziness, the settlers soon came to know the town as Kumara.

Punakaiki

Punakaiki, on the South Island's West Coast, is famous for its nearby rocks and blowholes. The rocks, which draw thousands of tourists to the area every year, are made up of hundreds of layers of limestone. The stratified layers resemble great big stacks of thin pancakes, and are consequently known as the Pancake Rocks.

Given that European settlers changed Maori names to suit their purposes, and Maori altered English words to fit the structure of their language, it seems obvious that Punakaiki is a Maori version of the word pancake, the word the Europeans used to describe the rocks. This all seems quite straightforward, apart from the fact that it is not true.

The Maori name for the rocks is indeed misspelled, but it has nothing to do with breakfast food. The word 'puna' means a spring of water. 'Kaiki' is thought to be a misspelling of 'kaike', which means to lie heaped one above another — an accurate description of the rocks. 'Puna' is therefore likely to be a reference to the booming blowholes that blast water skywards when there are big ocean swells.

The local Kai Tahu people have another meaning for the name Punakaiki. To them Punakaiki means the human neck and throat, which are represented by the rocks and the blowholes. The blowholes, like a human throat, spit water at a high speed when conditions are rough!

Nightcaps

One of Southland's most interesting European settlers is thought to be responsible for one of that province's most intriguing placenames. After stowing away on a voyage from England to Australia, John Howell worked his passage to New Zealand on a whaling ship. After working with Johnny Jones at Waikouaiti, Howell established a whaling station at the mouth of the Aparima River, then known as Jacob River, in the 1830s.

Following the downturn in the whaling trade Howell gave up whaling and focused his energies on farming the large parcel of land he had acquired in the area. Despite the closure of the whaling station the village that had grown up around it remained, and is today known as Riverton.

By the time he gave up whaling, Howell had been joined by other members of his family who had emigrated from England. The family was a large one. Two of Howell's half-sisters and their husbands came to live with him, along with his two stepbrothers. Captain Howell also had two children with his first wife, and a staggering seventeen children with his second wife. With all of this family in tow it is perhaps unsurprising that Riverton thrived.

It is said that it was while John Howell was travelling from Riverton to Bowmont Station with his brother-in-law, John Paulin, and his stepbrothers, William and George Stevens, that he endowed part of Southland with one of its oddest placenames. The tops of the Takitimu Mountains that dominate the northern Southland landscape were characteristically shrouded in a light mist. When one of the party commented on the mist, John Howell's reply was reportedly,

71
Double Meanings

'They have their nightcaps on.'

When a town sprang up in the area to support the growing coalmining industry, Howell's comment about the Takitimu Mountains was remembered and the town took the name Nightcaps.

Raglan

For all the knitters out there, Raglan can only mean one thing: a sleeve that goes right to the neckline of a jersey instead of being sewn into the shoulder of the garment. But mention Raglan to a surfer and it won't be sleeves they think of — it will be the wicked left-hand break at Manu Bay just out of Raglan in the Waikato.

Neither the sleeve nor the surf break have anything to do with how the town got its name though. That honour goes to a British military leader who was responsible for one of the most famous defeats ever suffered by the British army.

When the first European settlers arrived at the foot of Mount Karioi in 1854 the British Army was embroiled in the Crimean War. Around the time the settlers arrived from Taranaki the disastrous Charge of the Light Brigade was taking place in the Crimea. Without wishing to expand the knitting reference unduly, the battle took place at Balaclava and the troops were led by Lord Cardigan. But it was Fitzroy Somerset, Lord Raglan, who as commander in chief of the British Army sent the Light Brigade of 673 men into a valley that had numerous Russian soldiers on either side. The brigade lost 118 men and 326 horses in a futile and ill-organised attack. The battle also served as inspiration for Alfred, Lord Tennyson's classic poem, 'The Charge of the Light Brigade'.

Despite orchestrating this disastrous battle, Lord Raglan was still seen as a fitting figure after whom the new Waikato town should be named, and Raglan it has remained. In an ironic aside for fans of Raglan's left-hand surf break, Lord Raglan lost his right arm following injuries he sustained at the Battle of Waterloo and had to learn how to carry out tasks such as writing with his left hand.

Gore

To many people, gore is what you expect to see if you go to a horror movie. But ask most New Zealanders what gore means to them and you'll get a different answer. Chances are, if they are North Islanders they might mention the Gold Guitars, if they are from the South Island they'll probably talk about fishing, and if they are Southlanders they'll tell you about the Hokonui moonshine and the pie cart.

The town of Gore sits on the banks of the Mataura River, and it was from the river that it got its original name of Long Ford. A shallow section of the river provided one of the few relatively safe places for early settlers to cross the river. This crossing was soon host to a hotel and stables, and the village grew from there. On one side of the river the town of Gordon developed, and on the other side was Long Ford. While the name Long Ford was soon superseded by Gore, it has lived on in the suburb and schools that are called Longford to this day. The name Gordon also disappeared when the river was bridged and the two towns became one, which was named Gore.

The people of Long Ford were less than thrilled when their town's name was changed in 1863. The new name, Gore, was a tribute to Colonel Thomas Gore-Browne, who had just finished a five-year stint as Governor of New Zealand. Gore-Browne was an Englishman with an Irish family, who married in Scotland and joined a Welsh regiment. When he arrived in New Zealand as Governor he inherited a dysfunctional government and a colony on the verge of civil war.

Given that Gore-Browne's primary focus during his tenure as Governor was on relations between settlers and Maori in the North Island, and gaining more land for European settlers in the north, it is perhaps a little ironic that a town at the other end of the country should end up sporting his name. However, it would be interesting to ask the opinion of those who witnessed the battles that took place as a result of Gore-Browne's determination to purchase land at Waitara, in Taranaki — they may well have agreed that Gore is an appropriate name for a town that commemorates the man who could have prevented some of the bloodiest battles in New Zealand history.

Huia

The settlement of Huia sits on the edge of the Manukau Harbour, tucked in at the foot of the Waitakere Ranges. When you get there it is hard to believe you are mere minutes away from this country's biggest city.

At first sight, the name Huia appears to be drawn from the extinct New Zealand bird of the same name. Five hundred years ago the huia would have been found throughout the North Island, including in the forest around the town that now bears its name. The town was not named directly after the bird, however. It takes its name from a Maori chief, Te Huia, who camped in the area to take advantage of the plentiful supplies of fish that were available in the Manukau Harbour during the fishing season. Te Huia liked the harbourside spot so much he decided to stay on.

The name appears in early European records as Te Rau o Te Huia, which was translated as 'the treasured possession of Te Huia'. Rau doesn't translate as treasured possession, but the meaning could be 'plume or feather'. Maori believe the huia to be sacred and it is a huge honour to wear the tail feather of a huia. For Te Huia, the chief, a huia feather would have been a treasured possession.

The mana that was attached to the huia feathers meant they were extremely sought after and bird numbers dwindled. When Europeans arrived, many of the birds were killed and stuffed for museum collections. Then, in 1902, the Duke of York was given a huia feather in Rotorua. He put it on his hat, thus creating a huge demand for the feathers that effectively guaranteed the bird's extinction. The last live huia was sighted in 1907.

Cityscape

The majority of New Zealanders live in a handful of cities. While they probably read, write or say the name of their city multiple times in a day, a lot of people have no idea about the origin of the name. Here are the stories behind six of those city names.

Auckland

Auckland has established itself as New Zealand's main business centre, so it seems somewhat apt that the city's name was bestowed on it as thanks for a business deal.

New Zealand's first governor, Lieutenant William Hobson, fresh from orchestrating the signing of the Treaty of Waitangi, was given the task of selecting a capital for the colony. Until this time the town of Kororareka/Russell had served as the administrative centre of New Zealand. Colonial powers in Australia made it clear to Hobson that they were not at all keen for the capital to remain in Russell so he went in search of other possible locations from which to govern the new nation. Hobson soon chose a site on the Waitemata Harbour to serve as the new capital city. The land was acquired from the local Ngati Whatua people and a ceremony to commemorate the foundation of the new city was held on 18 September 1840.

The city's name was chosen by William Hobson in honour of his patron George Eden, 1st Earl of Auckland. The earl had long promoted Hobson's cause, and during a period as First Lord of the Admiralty he gave Hobson his first captaincy — that of HMS *Rattlesnake*, which was headed to the East Indies. Eden was then appointed Governor-General of India, where he embarked on a disastrous war in Afghanistan. On his return to England he once again took on the role of First Lord of the Admiralty, which he held until his death in 1849.

Back in New Zealand, immigrants began to flow into the town named after the earl. Within a year 2000 people were living in Auckland. Ships started arriving directly from Britain in 1842, the same year that royal approval for the name Auckland was announced.

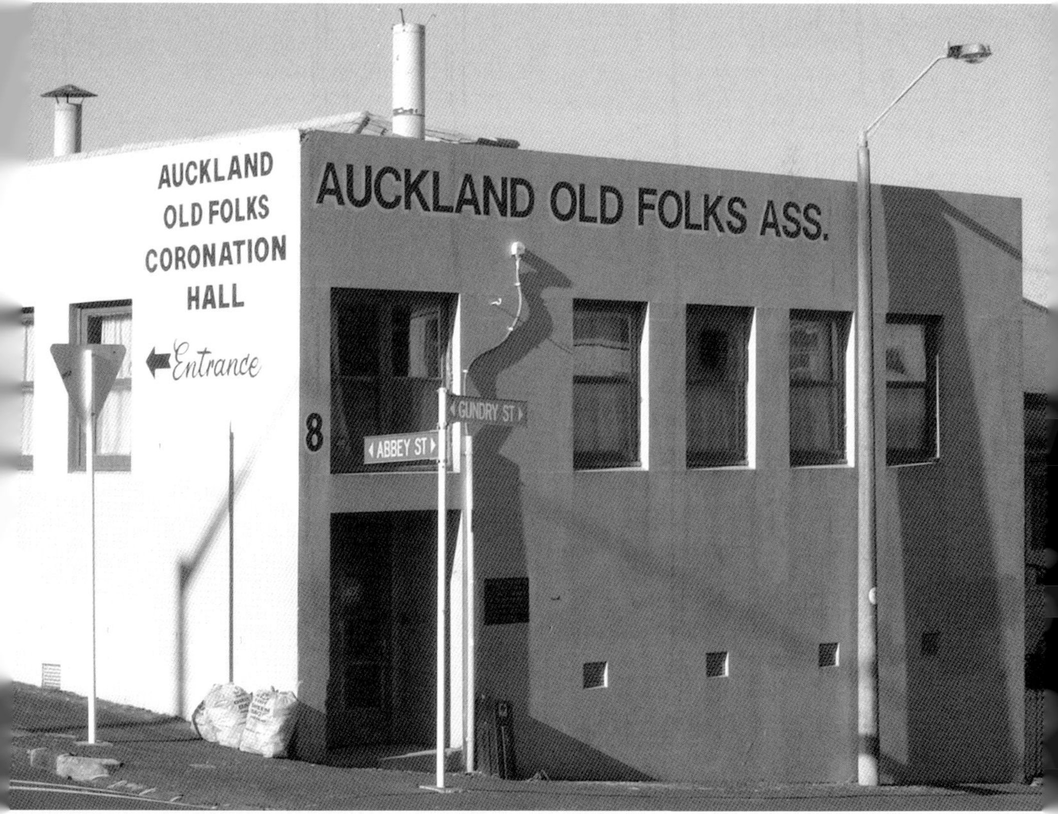

79
Cityscape

Hamilton

The peaceful rural scenes of grazing cattle that you see when you drive through the Waikato today would have been unthinkable to Maori and European alike during the New Zealand Wars. The main centre of the Waikato, Hamilton, was very much a product of the furious fighting that went on in the area. On 24 August 1864, the gunboat *Rangiriri* sailed up the Waikato River. Once it reached a Maori village called Kirikiriroa (meaning 'long stretches of gravel') a party of 118 men came ashore. Each of the men, who belonged to the 4th Waikato Regiment of the militia, was allocated a quantity of farmland and a section in town.

In keeping with the military beginnings of the town, the inhabitants named it after one of their own. Captain Fane Charles Hamilton was the commanding officer on HMS *Esk*, and was commander of the British naval brigade that amassed off Tauranga prior to the Battle of Gate Pa. Fighting began on 29 April 1864 and Captain Hamilton was soon called on to lead in the naval reserve force to support the soldiers and artillery units already at the pa. He survived only three days of fighting before being killed on 2 May 1864. Later that year the commanding officer of the 4th Waikato Regiment, Colonel Moule, decided that the new settlement at Kirikiriroa should be called Hamilton, as a mark of respect to his old colleague.

Wellington

It seems appropriate that our capital city is named after a leading nineteenth-century military leader and politician. It is also fitting that that person's name is synonymous with that most Kiwi item of footwear — the gumboot.

This unusual combination of attributes comes together in the person of Arthur Wellesley, 1st Duke of Wellington, British leader of military forces and briefly prime minister of the United Kingdom. Wellesley really made a name for himself as commander of the forces that defeated Napoleon at Waterloo. When he was raised to the peerage it was as Viscount, then Earl, then Marquess, and finally Duke of Wellington in the English county of Somerset.

Like many other New Zealand towns, Wellington was the brainchild of William and Edward Gibbon Wakefield and the New Zealand Company. After initially considering a site in the Marlborough Sounds, William Wakefield chose an area of Port Nicholson for the new town, and first arrived there in 1839 to acquire land for British settlement. The figurehead on Wakefield's ship, the *Tory*, depicted the Iron Duke, and soon after his arrival Wakefield bestowed the name Wellington on the harbour. Given the Duke's high profile in political circles, it is likely that Wakefield's salute to him would have helped the New Zealand Company gain continued support from the Duke and his compatriots.

It was only a few months before settlers began to arrive, and at first they settled in a town they called Britannia, in what is now known as Petone. However, the Hutt River was soon to change their plans. A serious flood saw not only a need for Wellington boots but also the destruction of huts and property, sending the settlers off in search of other, safer sites. They found one at Lambton Harbour and relocated to Wellington, although not quite the Wellington we know today — much of the heart of today's city is built on land raised through reclamation, and would have been underwater when the settlers first arrived.

Christchurch

Despite the Colonial Office rejecting plans for a purely Anglican settlement in the South Island, the Canterbury Association had religion at its core. It is not surprising then that the main town of this new settlement came to be called Christchurch.

The Canterbury Association developed out of the friendship between Edward Gibbon Wakefield and John Robert Godley in London. Wakefield hoped that New Zealand would become the foremost Anglican country in the world, while Godley foresaw the collapse of the church in England and viewed the new settlement as providing the church with a chance to regenerate.

They soon gathered plenty of support for their planned settlement throughout the church in England — the first president of the Canterbury Association was the Archbishop of Canterbury, Dr J.B. Sumner, and among the original members of the association were two archbishops and seven bishops, as well as a swathe of titled Englishmen and members of the House of Lords.

The name Christchurch was first suggested by John Robert Godley, as he was an old boy of Christ Church college at Oxford. The college was founded as Cardinal's College by Cardinal Wolsey in 1524, but was taken over by Henry VIII in 1529. When he re-established it in 1546 its name was changed to Christ Church. Since then the college has produced numerous prominent figures, including thirteen British prime ministers, the writers W.H. Auden and Lewis Carroll, and the philosopher John Locke. Many of the Canterbury Association's supporters were also old boys of this illustrious institution.

The name was not immediately accepted, with the Colonists' Society in London asking that the main town of the new settlement be named after association supporter Lord Lyttelton. However, Godley was to get his way, and Lyttelton is remembered in the province's main port.

With the name decided upon and political and financial wrangling done, the first Canterbury Association immigrants arrived in 1850 on four ships, the *Randolph*, *Charlotte Jane*, *Sir George Seymour* and *Cressy*. In keeping with the religious nature of the association each of the new Cantabrians was carefully vetted, and all were required to have certificates from the ministers of their parishes vouching for their sobriety, industriousness, honesty and respectability — all traits that are much admired in the city to this day.

Dunedin

The most Scottish town outside of Scotland — that is Dunedin's boast. Half of the city's suburbs are named after places in Scotland. A Dunedinite visiting Edinburgh is immediately struck by the presence of such familiar landmarks as Calton Hill, Princes Street, Canongate, Leith, Corstophine, Waverley, George Street and Moray Place. So it is only fitting that Dunedin's name hails not only from Scotland, but from Edinburgh.

The settlement was originally known as New Edinburgh as a nod to its roots. However, in October 1843 the Scottish publisher William Chambers wrote a letter to the *New Zealand Journal* suggesting that the new town be known as Dunedin to avoid a proliferation of 'news', which he saw as an abomination. Chambers' suggested name was derived from Dùn Êideann, an early Gaelic form of Edinburgh, which originally meant the fortress of Êideann.

The suggestion was not taken up immediately. New Edinburgh remained in usage, as did the 'Otago settlement', and the Maori name for the area, Otakau (the term anglicised to form the province's name, Otago). Eventually, however, the new name gained more support, including the approval of the Reverend Thomas Burns, who was one of the leaders of the Lay Association of the Free Church of Scotland. This breakaway group from the Presbyterian church saw settlement in the new colonies as an answer to the grinding poverty of the old country.

Charles Kettle, whose name now graces a rugby ground, created the original plans for Dunedin in 1845, under instructions from the New Zealand Company. Kettle's plans included the Octagon as the centre of the as yet unbuilt town, and one imagines he would be happy to know that over 160 years later the city still gravitates around the Octagon.

With the name decided upon and the plans drawn up, the city was finally settled by immigrants from the Free Church of Scotland's first two ships, the *John Wickliffe* and the *Philip Lang*, which arrived at Port Chalmers in early 1848. To this day the city celebrates its Scottish ancestry with a Dunedin tartan, locally made haggis and the skirl of bagpipes in the hills.

Invercargill

Invervegas, Invergiggle or just plain Invers — Invercargill gets called all these things and a few more. If a handful of city councillors had had their way none of these names would exist.

In 1930 the councillors proposed that Invercargill's name be changed to plain 'Cargill'. One of their reasons for suggesting the change was that Invercargill 'was not a euphonious name', but more than this they objected to the way in which the name had been bestowed on their town.

Roll back to 1856, and head north to Dunedin. On 7 January 1856 Governor Thomas Gore-Browne was invited to a banquet hosted by Captain William Cargill, leader of the Free Church settlement of Dunedin. The settlers of Dunedin had been buying farmland in the south and were keen to establish a port in the region. While the port was established at Bluff, the main township was situated further to the north. Gore-Browne wanted to pay tribute to his host in Dunedin, and asked that the town be named Invercargill. The councillors who later suggested the change believed that Gore-Browne had first suggested the name as a joke, and they didn't appreciate the fact that their town was named as the result of a jape. Their recommendation was opposed, however.

The name Invercargill is thought by many to be a misnomer. Inver is most commonly taken to derive from a Gaelic word meaning the mouth of the river, which would mean Invercargill means 'at the mouth of the Cargill River'. Since there is no Cargill River, the name is meaningless. However, inver can also mean the meeting of the waters. The Oreti and Makarewa rivers join north of the city and flow out to the estuary on Invercargill's outskirts, where they are joined by the waters of the Waihopai River — so Invercargill can be translated to mean 'Cargill where the waters meet'.

Double the Fun

6

In New Zealand we have our own version of the question, 'What came first — the chicken or the egg?' In our case it is, 'What came first — Palmerston or Palmerston?' There are two (or in one case three) places for each of the names in this section — one in the North Island and one in the South Island. Some have had 'North' or 'South' appended to their names at some stage to distinguish them from each other, but which did come first? Read on . . .

Havelock/Havelock North

1857 was the key year for the establishment of two New Zealand towns — Havelock and Havelock North. Both towns date back to that year, and the man they were named after has that year engraved on his tombstone.

Havelock North in Hawke's Bay is truly a town of wine and honey, both being produced in quantities there. It was called Havelock until 1866, when the North was added to distinguish it from its southern equivalent. Havelock in Marlborough, on the other hand, was built on gold. During the gold rushes of the mid-1800s the town boasted a staggering 23 hotels. Now the gold has gone, Havelock is primarily a fishing town.

Both towns were named after Sir Henry Havelock in the late 1850s, with the northern version having its name bestowed by Alfred Dommett, who served as a magistrate in Hawke's Bay and later became MP for Nelson, then Premier of New Zealand.

Havelock is another of the many New Zealand placenames that has its origins in India. Sir Henry Havelock was a British soldier who first arrived in India in 1823. He was involved in a number of campaigns, including the First Anglo-Burmese War and the First Afghan War, but it was in India that he spent most of his career. He gradually worked his way up through the ranks of the army, eventually becoming an adjutant-general in 1857. Havelock spent part of that year commanding a division in Persia but arrived back in India in time for the outbreak of the Indian rebellion. He led a division across Uttar Pradesh and despite being outnumbered defeated insurgents throughout the region.

Lucknow was also under siege from militants, and the British forces there were surrounded. Havelock led several attempts to break the siege, and finally succeeded on 25 September. His victory was fêted throughout the British empire, but before a month was out Lucknow had been recaptured and relieved again and Havelock, the war hero, had rather unglamorously succumbed to a fatal bout of dysentery.

Waimate/Waimate North

Both of New Zealand's Waimates have famous immigrants. Waimate in the North is famous as the site of one of this country's first European mission stations. On a completely different tack, the southern version of Waimate is famous for being home to a large wild wallaby population.

The name Waimate means the same thing in both cases. Wai is water, and mate means stagnant or sluggish. One of the few things the towns have in common is that they were both built near swampy land, which accounts for their names.

Canterbury's version of Waimate was originally called Te Waimatemate, which means exactly the same as Waimate. For many years the area served as a camp for Maori, who would stay for several months at a time, making the most of the abundant natural resources available. European settlement began with Michael Studholme, who arrived in 1854 and established Te Waimate run. Studholme's first home, the Cuddy Cottage, is still standing and continues to be maintained by his descendants. Sawmilling and farming were the two main industries that underpinned the settlement of Waimate, and they remain vital to the town's economy to this day.

Waimate in the North Island lies inland from Paihia. It is close to Lake Omapere, and surrounded by a number of streams; the abundance of waterways providing the reason for its name. To distinguish it from Waimate in Canterbury, it is often called Waimate North. Samuel Marsden established a mission station in Waimate North in 1831. While there were several other Christian stations in New Zealand by that stage, Waimate North was the first inland mission station.

The idea behind the establishment of the settlement was that local Maori could be introduced to Anglicanism at the same time as being taught how to farm and produce food. The people of the area realised that if they wanted to learn the skills of the new arrivals they would have to take the religious education that came with it. A thriving community was soon based at Waimate, including a school, a church and a mission house. However, when the church leaders agreed to allow Waimate to be used by British troops fighting Hone Heke in 1845 much of the Maori congregation left the mission, disillusioned by the political stance taken by the church.

A presence was maintained at Waimate North well into the twentieth century but today only one building from the original settlement remains — the Mission House.

Kinloch

Kinloch is a Gaelic word which means head of the lake, kin being head and loch being lake. There are three towns called Kinloch in New Zealand alone. Around the world there are hundreds of them.

The most peculiar of the New Zealand Kinlochs is the one in

Double the Fun

Canterbury. It lies three kilometres from the settlement of Little River, but it doesn't lie on the banks of a lake. It is instead in the middle of Banks Peninsula. The reason it is called Kinloch is that it was named by Hugh Buchanan who hailed from the town of Kinloch Mhor in the Scottish county of Argyllshire.

A bit further south in Otago's Lakes District lies the second Kinloch — on the western side of the top end of Lake Wakatipu, opposite the town of Glenorchy. Today the settlement is a shadow of its former self, when it was a thriving sawmilling town. Now the town attracts tourists who are keen on the outdoors, as it lies near the start of the Routeburn and Greenstone tracks. The name Kinloch was suggested for the town by a Scottish settler in the 1860s. Mary Bryant arrived in central Otago in 1860 and settled near the head of Lake Wakatipu. She suggested the name Kinloch be used, as the land around the top of the lake reminded her of the Scottish highlands.

Further north and almost a century later, the third Kinloch was born. In 1953, Keith Holyoake, who later became a long-serving prime minister, then governor-general, and his business partner Ian Gibbs bought a large tract of scrub-covered land that backed on to Lake Taupo. Part of the land was converted into farmland and part was subdivided for housing. The land lay in the Whangamata Valley, but to avoid confusion with Whangamata in the Coromandel, they decided to call their planned village Kinloch. It lies about 20 kilometres from Taupo.

The first streets were developed in 1959, the marina following a year later. The link between Holyoake and the town is still evident today, with many of the streets named after his family. Being the preferred holiday spot of a top politician brought the fledgling town plenty of attention and the early residents of Kinloch were happy to think that their town was the summertime capital of the nation. Like its counterpart in Otago, Kinloch on Lake Taupo still attracts plenty of tourists. It is famed for its trout fishing and an exclusive golfing resort.

Lake Rotoiti

The actual meaning of the name Rotoiti is simple — it's the stories of how the lakes were named that are more complex. Lake Rotoiti in the North Island lies just next to Lake Rotorua on the volcanic plateau. The South Island's Lake Rotoiti is 64 kilometres from Nelson and is part of the Nelson Lakes National Park.

'Roto' means lake and 'iti' means small, which is probably appropriate for the South Island lake, but the North Island one is quite big. Regardless of their size, both lakes are favourite spots for people keen on trout fishing and tramping.

According to taha Maori, Lake Rotoiti was dug by the great explorer Rakaihautu, who was head of the *Uruao* canoe that brought the Waitaha people to Aotearoa. While travelling through the South Island, Rakaihautu was feeling a bit thirsty. There were no water sources around so he thrust his ko, or digging stick, into the ground. Like magic a pool of fresh, clear water came bubbling up from the ground. This was the first of many lakes that Rakaihautu formed in the South Island.

The name Rotoiti was first recorded by Europeans in 1843. The explorer John Cotterill noted the lake's existence and wrote its name as Roto Iti. The same year Charles Heaphy named it Lake Arthur, after Captain Arthur Wakefield, but this name didn't last long. By 1846 it had fallen from use and Rotoiti was accepted as the name of the lake.

In the North Island, Rotoiti is a shortened version of Te Roto iti kite a Ihenga, which means 'the small lake seen by Ihenga'. In the mid-fourteenth century, Ihenga was out looking for food for his pregnant wife. One of Ihenga's dogs was chasing a kiwi and ended up diving into the lake, where it caught and ate some fish. His master wondered where the dog had been when it returned all wet. When the dog then threw up the fish Ihenga was curious as to where it had got them. Eventually the dog led him through the dense forest to the lake.

When he arrived there, Ihenga found the lake abundant with fish, eels and freshwater crayfish. He was delighted to find heaps of food and fresh water all in one place, and he named the lake Te Roto iti kite a Ihenga so that he and his descendants would be able to use it from then on.

Palmerston/Palmerston North

The Palmerston conundrum is one that causes consternation on a daily basis. Meet people who say they come from Palmerston and it's unclear whether they mean the one in Manawatu in the North Island or the one in Otago in the South Island.

The history of the name Palmerston is one that, in some ways, reflects the development of the country. Palmerston in Otago was surveyed and named in 1864. Its North Island counterpart received the name Palmerston in 1866 (despite the fact that the first settlers didn't arrive there until 1871).

At the time Otago was in the throes of the gold rushes and the consequent economic power that came with them. Dunedin was the main financial centre of the country, and so the southern Palmerston retained its name, and temporarily used the suffix South. Its northern sibling had to take on the suffix North in 1871 following continual postal confusion at having two towns with the same name.

Just as the financial heart of the country moved north, the northern version of Palmerston grew into a city while the southern version remains a small provincial town (albeit one that has some of the best pies in the country). Despite the fact the Palmerston North is thus named, most people who live there talk only of living in Palmerston, so the confusion at the post office really hasn't been solved.

Both towns were named after Henry John Temple, Viscount Palmerston, who was prime minister of Great Britain from 1855–58 and 1859–65. After entering parliament in 1807 Palmerston soon rose through the ranks of the Tory Party to become secretary-at-war just two years later, at the age of 25. Eventually Palmerston took on the role of foreign secretary, in which he concentrated on retaining peace in Europe against the threat of revolution. As home secretary Palmerston supported Britain's involvement in the Crimean War, and despite popular dissent over the nation's involvement in the war he became prime minister in 1855. The last years of his stewardship were marked as years of stability for Britain.

On a personal level, Palmerston was a somewhat abrasive man, earning the nickname 'Lord Pumice Stone'. However, he can't have rubbed everyone the wrong way as he also gained the nickname 'Lord Cupid' after being cited as a co-respondent in a divorce case at the age of 79.

The Shag Factor

7

Remember when you were a kid and you'd sit in the back seat of the car and howl with laughter over things you thought were a bit rude? Well, the placenames in this section will either make kids laugh or they'll give parents the ammunition they need so that when the giggling starts they can explain the real reason behind the so-called naughty names.

Waipu

When it comes to eliciting juvenile comments from the back seat there are not many places that can rival Waipu. Mention Waipu to anyone with a base sense of humour and you're almost guaranteed to garner the response 'Why not?' This kind of potty humour would not have gained the approval of Waipu's founding father, the Reverend Norman McLeod.

When McLeod and his followers arrived from Scotland, via Nova Scotia and Australia, in 1854, it was with the hope of establishing a Gaelic-speaking settlement that would be allowed to practise its own variety of Presbyterianism. They soon realised that the land at Waipu was good for farming, that the waters were good for fishing and that the New Zealand government would leave them to worship in peace.

The first settlers established their town on the banks of the Waipu River, just near where five streams converge into the river. It is this river that gives the town of Waipu its name. While 'wai' means water, 'pu' has several meanings. With all the streams criss-crossing the land around Waipu, the most likely meaning of pu here is 'murmuring'. The name Waipu would then evoke the whispering sound that running water often makes.

There are, however, a couple of other possible meanings of Waipu. Pu also relates to guns, and some people claim Waipu means water that sounds like gunfire. There is also a theory that Waipu means reddening water, which could refer to the sea off the coast of Waipu. Perhaps this name was given to Waipu when the water was host to one of those brightly coloured algal blooms.

Whatever the meaning of Waipu, the answer will always be 'Why not?'

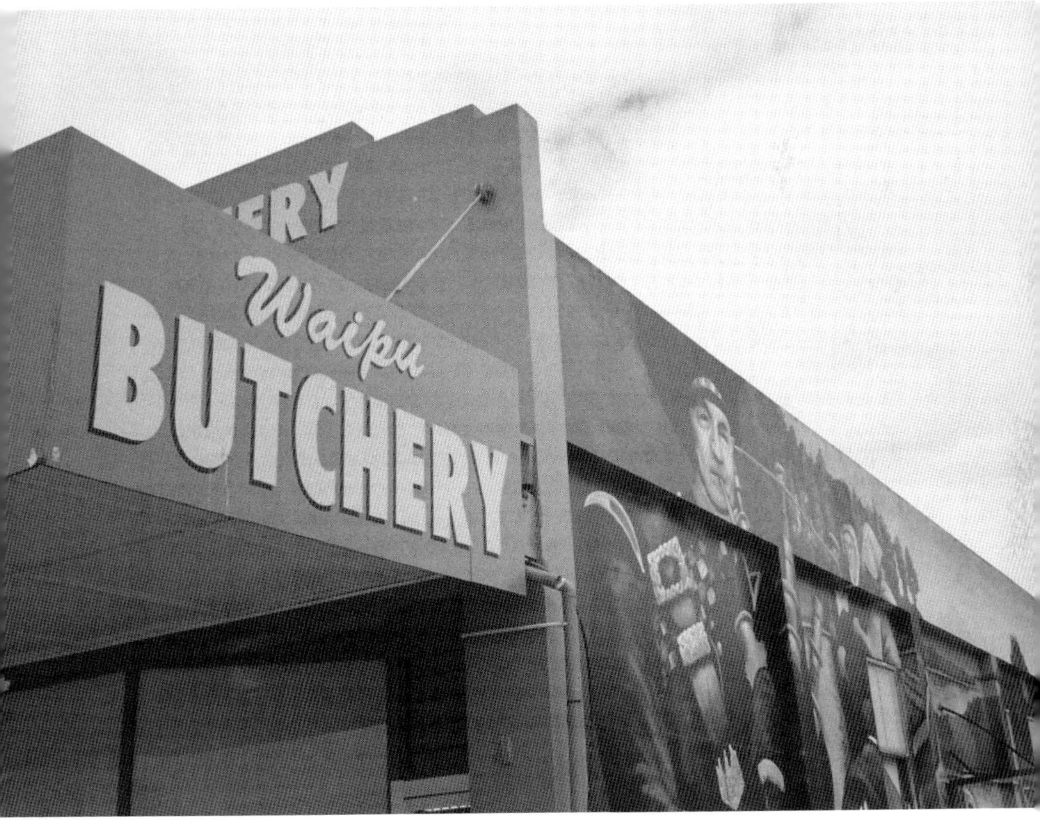
ERY
Waipu
BUTCHERY

Mount Tarawera

The volcanic plateau of the central North Island is home to some of New Zealand's most spectacular sights. And there are none more spectacular than the plumes of smoke that can sometimes be seen issuing from the area's volcanoes. One of these volcanoes, Mount Tarawera, is the subject of some debate as to the origin of its name.

Tarawera, you see, can have several different meanings, all of which can easily be justified by whoever is telling the story. There is no doubt about the fact that 'wera' means burn or burnt. It's the meaning of 'tara' that's the cause of all the trouble. One possible meaning is peak, thereby giving a definition of burnt peak. Given that in 1886 Mount Tarawera was the scene of one of this country's most devastating eruptions, it certainly is a burnt peak.

However, Tarawera can also mean burnt spear. The story goes that Hikawera, a chief from Hawke's Bay, had come to the central plateau to hunt birds. He had a fantastic hunting season, and when he left he stored his spears in a hut in the area in readiness for the next hunting season. When he returned the following year, however, the hut had been burnt down and his spears had burned with it.

The third, and most snicker-inducing, meaning of Tarawera is if you take tara to mean vagina. Was the mountain named after the pool of burning lava at its centre?

Be it a spear, a peak or a woman's genitals, the one thing we do know about Tarawera is that something got burnt.

Urewera

Urewera country is one of the last natural wildernesses in New Zealand. Home of the Tuhoe people, the Children of the Mist, the Urewera has a reputation as being mysterious and magical.

The region's name adds to the mystery, as 'wera' means to burn, and 'ure' means penis. The region and the national park that shares its name are thus called 'singed genitals'. The story behind the name is one of tragedy.

Murakeke, of Nga Potiki, and his two sons, Tama Kaimoana and Tuhoe Potiki, were making their way across the Kaingaroa plains after losing a battle. As they neared the Whakatane River, Murakeke decided to stop and rest for a little while. They had no food with them so, in desperation, Murakeke ordered his people to kill a sacred dog and cook it — an action that was bound to bring bad luck.

Murakeke asked that the best parts be fed to his youngest son, but Tuhoe Potiki got only the ears, while his older brother, Tama Kaimoana, ate well. When Murakeke came to find out why Tuhoe Potiki was crying, then told Tama Kaimoana off, both the boys gave him a really hard time. Following on the heels of a defeat in battle, Murakeke couldn't cope with being made fun of by his beloved children. He had a fit and fell into the fire, where he suffered severe burns, not just to his penis, but to his whole body. Indeed, the burns were so severe that Murakeke died.

Tutaekuri River

Kids love to learn 'naughty' words in as many languages as possible. In New Zealand that means they are likely to know that 'tutae' is the Maori word for excrement. Put that together with the fact that 'kuri' means dog and you've got a story that's bound to pique their interest. The Tutaekuri River flows from the Kaweka Ranges out to sea near Napier. But how on earth did the people of Hawke's Bay get a river that seems to be called dog poo?

About 400 years ago, the people of Ngati Kahungunu from Wairoa heard that there was heaps of food to be had near Porangahau. They set off on the trek to the coast, but when they got there they found there wasn't much food to be had at all and they had to turn around and walk all the way home again. They were absolutely starving by the time they reached Hikawera's pa, which lies between Waiohiki and Omahu. Hikawera decided to have a feast, and make sure his visitors didn't leave his home hungry. He ordered his people to kill seventy dogs in order to feed the travellers.

There's a spot on the river that's now called Te Umukuri, which denotes the ovens where the dogs were cooked. Once they had eaten, the group from Ngati Kahungunu set off for home and Hikawera's people threw the offal from the dogs into the river. Hence the name Tutaekuri — the offal of the dogs.

Blackball

The town of Blackball on the West Coast is probably best known for its history of protest. The town's miners striked to gain a 30-minute lunchbreak — an event that is said to have led to the establishment of the Federation of Labour and the New Zealand Labour Party — the country's Communist Party was based there for a time, and more recently the Blackball Hilton got into a stoush with the hotel chain of the same name and is now known as 'Formerly the Blackball Hilton'.

But where does the somewhat testicular name Blackball come from? Much like everything else in the town, its name sprang forth from the mining industry. The town was originally called Moonlight Gully after George Fairweather Moonlight, the Scottish prospector whose flamboyant attire made him a noticeable feature on the local goldfields.

While Moonlight is linked to gold, it was coal that led to the town being called Blackball. When coal was discovered on the Coast, land became sought after. One parcel of land on the banks of the Grey River was bought by a British shipping company. That company was the Black Ball Shipping Line. Owned by James Baines and Co. of Liverpool, the company was one of the main carriers of emigrants and cargo to Australia during the gold rushes. Of all the shipping lines Black Ball is said to have brought more emigrants to Australia than any other.

Once the gold rushes had subsided the company relied on mail delivery contracts and diversifying its routes. This wasn't enough to save it from financial ruin and by 1873 the company was broke, its name only living on in history books and a lively town on New Zealand's West Coast.

Pigroot

Driving across the Pigroot when we were kids, we thought it was hilarious when we saw a pighunter piggybacking a dead pig on the Pigroot. We went on about it until Dad threatened to put us out to run behind. It was not until years later that the origins of the name Pigroot became the subject of any sort of smutty mirth in the back seat.

The Pigroot is the name of the road that connects North Otago to the Maniototo Plains in that province's hinterland. It was established as a supply route for the goldfields of Central Otago in the mid-nineteenth century. Back then the road was rough going, with the summit rising to 640 metres above sea level. As a result of the dodgy road conditions, there is some speculation that the name was given to the route by travellers disgusted at the tough going they encountered.

Another theory suggests that the area used to be rife with feral pigs that scratched around in the ground trying to find juicy speargrass roots to eat. The most likely theory on how the Pigroot got its name is down to John Turnbull Thomson, who endowed the Maniototo with many of its animalesque names, such as the Sowburn, the Eweburn and the Hogburn.

Thomson used the pass to cross into Central Otago when he was surveying the province in 1857. On his way across the Pigroot he encountered some animals that were not used to seeing humans and were therefore not intimidated by them. One of these creatures was an inquisitive feral boar that came nose to nose with Thomson's horse. While that's the pig part of the equation sewn up, the root part is a little more elusive. One possible explanation is that 'root' has replaced the original word 'route' in the name.

Dagg Sound

If someone calls you a bit of a dag, then that's a compliment, right? But when you think about it, what they could be saying is that you're a bit of crusty old sheep's excrement . . . and that's not a compliment in anyone's language!

OK, so we know what a dag is, but have you ever wondered what one sounds like? South of Doubtful Sound in Fiordland lies a fiord called Dagg Sound. While many Kiwis would like it to be named after sheep poo, or after that classic Kiwi comic Fred Dagg, it's not. In 1804, Captain William Dagg was captain of the whaling ship the *Scorpion*. He had been working as a whaler in the south of the South Island and was heading back to Sydney with a cargo of sperm whale oil. Before heading back across the Tasman he decided to divert in to one of the fiords on the west coast.

Southern Maori knew the fiord as Te Ra, or 'the sun'. It earned this name as it is open to more sunlight throughout the day than the other inlets along the coast. Dagg sailed into Te Ra and found a huge population of seals there. As seal skins were sought-after fashion items in the early 1800s, Dagg saw a chance to make some serious money and set about slaughtering the seals.

When William Dagg finally sailed into Sydney Harbour, the *Scorpion* was heaving with not only the whale oil but also with a massive 4759 seal skins, all of which were purloined from Te Ra. Dagg's massive haul from Fiordland became famous throughout the whaling and sealing stations of the Pacific, and the site of his seal slaughter soon inherited his name.

Cape Foulwind

New Zealand's smelliest placename is not to be found among the sulphur-scented towns of the North Island's geothermal wonderland, as you might expect. Rather, it is attached to a rocky promontory on the west coast of the South Island.

On 15 December 1642 Abel Tasman took a break from sailing along the west coast of the South Island and put in to shore near a rocky cape. As the first European visitor to the area, which now lies a 20-minute drive west of Westport, he decided to name the rocky cape. After a lot of thinking he gave it the original title Klippengen Hoek or, um, well, Rocky Cape.

One hundred and twenty-eight years later another European explorer, Captain James Cook, was in the neighbourhood. He was mapping the coast near Rocky Cape when his ship, *Endeavour*, sailed into difficult winds. The squally weather and unpredictable winds drove the ship some distance offshore and off course. Cook was less than thrilled at this unplanned diversion and the interruption to his charting of the coast, and he decided to rename Rocky Cape to commemorate his bad time. Thus he left the niffy name of Cape Foulwind on the coast.

Since its renaming by Cook, the Cape has managed to live up to its name by playing host to one of this country's most accessible colonies of fur seals (and if you're downwind from them you know about it) and is also home to the Star Tavern, which boasts that it is New Zealand's closest pub to Australia (and too much beer can indeed cause foul wind!).

Shag River

Tourists wielding cameras are a common sight around the South Island. Photographic souvenirs of their holidays usually feature lakes, rivers and mountains. But the signs on the bridges across one Otago river attract more than their fair share of camera-wielding British travellers.

That river, and its associated point, is the charmingly titled Shag. Of the definitions available, New Zealanders are likely to know the shag as a fish-eating, surface-diving seabird; our English cousins, however, know the shag primarily as something you hope to get after too many lagers down the pub after the footy on a Saturday night!

Rising in the Kakanui Range, the Shag River flows 50 kilometres to the sea near Palmerston in Otago. Unsurprisingly, the Shag River flows out to sea near Shag Point. Apart from the giggling tourists stopping to take pictures of the Shag River signs, the area's attractions include a seal colony, a yellow-eyed penguin population and stunning views of passing whales.

Readers will not be surprised to learn that Shag Point is also home to a huge population of shags. It is thought that both the Shag River and Shag Point were given their names in 1857 when John Turnbull Thomson was surveying North Otago. Had he been surveying the area many thousands of years earlier, it might have been called Plesiosaur Point after the dinosaurs whose bones were found nearby in 1983 — but perhaps the English tourists wouldn't find that quite so funny.

Bibliography

Andersen, Johannes, *Maori Place-Names*. Polynesian Society of New Zealand, Wellington, 1942.

Brooking, Tom. 'Cargill, William 1784–1860', *Dictionary of New Zealand Biography*. Updated 7 July 2005, http://www.dnzb.govt.nz/

Buchanan, J.D.H., *The Maori History & Place Names of Hawke's Bay*. A.H & A.W. Reed, Wellington, 1973.

Cowan, James, *The New Zealand Wars: A History of the Maori Campaigns and the Pioneering Period*. R.E. Owen, Wellington, 1955.

Dalton, B.J., 'Browne, Thomas Robert Gore 1807–1887', *Dictionary of New Zealand Biography*. Updated 7 July 2005, http://www.dnzb.govt.nz/

Evison, Harry C., 'Mackay, James 1831–1912', *Dictionary of New Zealand Biography*. Updated 7 July 2005, http://www.dnzb.govt.nz/

Fisher, Robin, 'Williams, Henry 1792–1867', *Dictionary of New Zealand Biography*. Updated 7 July 2005, http://www.dnzb.govt.nz/

Hall-Jones, John, *Fiordland Place-Names*. Fiordland National Park Board, Invercargill, 1979.

Hearn, T.J., 'Read, Thomas Gabriel 1824-1826?–1894', *Dictionary of New Zealand Biography*. Updated 7 July 2005, http://www.dnzb.govt.nz/

Insull, H.A.H., *Marlborough Place Names*. A.H. & A.W. Reed, Wellington, 1952.

Maling, Peter B., 'Haast, Johann Franz Julius von 1822–1887', *Dictionary of New Zealand Biography*. Updated 7 July 2005, http://www.dnzb.govt.nz/

McIntyre, W. David, 'FitzGerald, James Edward 1818–1896', *Dictionary of New Zealand Biography*. Updated 7 July 2005, http://www.dnzb.govt.nz

Owens, J.M.R., 'Taylor, Richard 1805–1873', *Dictionary of New Zealand Biography*. Updated 7 July 2005, http://www.dnzb.govt.nz/

Pope, D. & J., *Mobil New Zealand Travel Guide: North Island*. Reed Methuen, Wellington, 1986.
—— *Mobil New Zealand Travel Guide: South Island*. Reed Methuen, Wellington, 1983.
Reed, A.W., *Place Names of New Zealand*. A.H. & A.W. Reed, Wellington, 1979.
—— *Supplement to Place Names of New Zealand*. A.H. & A.W. Reed, Wellington, 1979.
—— *Reed Dictionary of Maori Place Names*. Reed, Auckland, 2003.
Riley, Murdoch, *Know Your South Island Place Names*. Viking Sevenseas, Paraparaumu, 1995.
Robinson, Roger. 'Butler, Samuel 1835–1902', *Dictionary of New Zealand Biography*. Updated 7 July 2005, http://www.dnzb.govt.nz/
Wilson, Eva, 'Howell, John 1810?–1874', *Dictionary of New Zealand Biography*. Updated 7 July 2005, http://www.dnzb.govt.nz/
Woodley, Suzanne, *The Native Townships Act 1895: Preliminary Report*. Waitangi Tribunal, Wellington, 1996.

Websites

www.christchurchartgallery.org.nz
www.geocities.com/scandannevirke/
www.helensville.co.nz
www.uppermoutere.school.nz
www.wikipedia.com

Acknowledgements:

A huge thanks to: Margaret and Brian McCloy, Vicki O'Connell, Didier Lionnet and Anne-Lise Serres; Sarah Ell and Rob Shaw for taking photos for me while they travelled the countryside; Nick Turzynski, Katy Yiakmis, Chris Coad, Susan Brierley, Jenny Hellen, Catherine O'Loughlin and Sarah (again) for their work on the book; and to my family, friends and colleagues who put up with me while I was writing it!

If you have a New Zealand place name story that you'd like to share please email it to whykick@gmail.com for possible inclusion in future collections.

Image credits:

Chris Coad: original image pages 10, 30, 46, 62, 76, 86, 96
Brian McCloy: pages 19, 24, 39, 67
Didier Lionnet and Anne-Lise Serres: pages 28, 43, 53, 57, 91
Nicola McCloy: page 33, 74, 79, 99
Sarah Ell: page 107
Vicki O'Connell: page 8, 71